OCR AS Religious Studies

Jewish Scriptures

Yitzchok Sliw

AuthorHouse™
1663 Liberty Drive
Bloomington, IN 47403
www.authorhouse.com
Phone: 1-800-839-8640

First published by AuthorHouse 08/02/2011

ISBN: 978-1-4567-8115-6 (sc)

authorHOUSE®

TABLE OF CONTENTS

BACKGROUND TO JEWISH SCRIPTURES

The texts listed are to be studied with reference to their date, authorship, purpose and historicity.

In discussing the texts candidates should be able to refer to their structure and theological importance as well as simply demonstrating knowledge of their content. Candidates should be able to comment in detail on the texts in relation to the concepts listed and consider the texts from a traditional Jewish or a critical approach.

The first part of the Jewish Scriptures syllabus deals with the controversial issue of external verification. It examines a number of studies made in the academic world to discover what evidence there is either to support or challenge the traditional explanations for the origins of the various texts that make up the Tenach.

For an Orthodox Jew, of course, external verification is unnecessary. The discussions and conclusions of the Talmud, together with the chronological records found in the Tenach itself are evidence enough. Some would say, therefore, that studying subjects such as charting the Time Line of Scriptures and Form Criticism is quite unnecessary.

Some Orthodox Jews would go even further and suggest that it was quite wrong to study these subjects. Those who conduct this research are usually not religious, often not even Jewish. At best, it could be said that they do not appreciate the nature of that which is Divinely inspired. In some cases, it may even be suspected that the very purpose of their research is to undermine the reverence with which these texts are approached in Orthodox circles.

On the other hand, some would say that the integrity of Orthodox Jewish scholarship demands that points raised by these studies be addressed. If everything in the Tenach is true, which is a fundamental principle of Orthodox Judaism, then no honest academic study could possibly contradict what is written in the Tenach.

In the pages that follow, we will look at some of the questions raised by scholars of literary analysis, archaeology, philology and history over the past two hundred years. We will also examine the Talmudic and Midrashic explanations for the origins and compilation of the Tenach as well as some research done by Orthodox Jewish archaeologists.

Does the study of subjects such as Form Criticism and the Time Line of the Tenach help us to better understand the Tenach?

That is for you to decide..........................

A TIMELINE
OF SCRIPTURES

PLACING JEWISH SCRIPTURES IN THEIR HISTORICAL CONTEXT AND CONSIDERING THE PROBABLE DATES OF PRINCIPAL EVENTS AND PEOPLE, I.E.:

THE LIFE OF ABRAHAM

THE LIFE OF MOSES

THE EXODUS

THE LIFE OF DAVID

THE LIFE OF ISAIAH

THE MACCABEAN REVOLT

THE DESTRUCTION OF THE TEMPLE

INTRODUCTION

The books of the Bible were not all written at the same time.

The Babylonian Talmud [Bava Bathra 14b-15a] contains a debate concerning authorship of the different books and its conclusions are accepted as true by Orthodox Jews.

The major historical source for the Orthodox Jewish belief regarding the historical sequence of the Biblical period is the Midrashic work *Seder Olam*. It follows the literal chronology of the Bible itself and attempts to resolve difficulties arising out of events not always being placed in their chronological sequence.

A scholarly twentieth century work, *Universal Jewish History* by *Philip Biberfeld*, attempts to demonstrate the relative accuracy of the Biblical record in relation to other historical and archaeological studies.

For Orthodox Jews, the Bible is the most authoritative of all documents and its narratives are all historically true. External evidence to verify the truth of the Biblical narratives is unnecessary.

Other scholars, however, take the view that whilst Biblical tales may well contain a true moral or ethical lesson, the narratives themselves may not necessarily be historically accurate.

WHAT ARE THE DIFFICULTIES IN ATTEMPTING TO DATE BIBLICAL EVENTS?

Historians and archeologists have encountered many problems in their attempts to date Biblical events accurately:

1. Lack of written evidence

Most of the documents of other nations living in the Middle East during the Biblical period have not survived, limiting the opportunities for external verification.

Archeologists have discovered cuneiform tablets from the Mesopotamian area, but with very little reference to Biblical events. With the notable exception of the Dead Sea scrolls, the relatively damp area that was inhabited by the Israelites has prevented most parchment scrolls from surviving to the modern day.

2. Strong Oral Tradition

Much of early Jewish tradition was transmitted orally; therefore documents may well have changed in form from when events actually happened until they were written down.

Also, two or more different historical events may have been woven into one story for the sake of its ethical or moral lesson. Historians have occasionally noticed narratives set in a certain time period with cultural or social features relevant to a later period, which indicates some 'constructive editing' had taken place.

3. Historical Bias

All historical records are written according to the views of their author. For example, in the U.S.A., historians talk of the revolution that overthrew the British in 1776. In England, it used to be taught that their colony was 'granted' its independence after demonstrating its desire and ability to govern itself! Similarly, all ancient historical documents must be treated carefully if the 'historical bias' of the author is unknown. Orthodox scholars would say this point does not apply to the Tenach because it was Divinely written or inspired.

4. The Bible Is Not A History Book

The purpose of the Bible is to teach the principles of religion, the nature of G-d, the moral and ethical path that a human being, particularly a Jew, should follow. Its authors were not necessarily concerned with historical details and many narratives are not specifically identified as being from a particular time period.

There is a Talmudic principle that 'there is no chronological sequence to the Bible'. Now the Bible clearly does follow a general chronological sequence. This is usually understood to mean that, even though the Bible proceeds chronologically, if a lesson can be learned by moving narratives out of their historical order, then this will be done. For example, in Genesis, the death of Terach (Abraham's father) is recorded before G-d's first prophetic communication with Abraham. Terach was 70 when Abraham was born[1] and died aged 205[2]. Yet Abraham was 75 when G-d first spoke to him[3].

---

1   Genesis 11:26
2   ibid. v.32
3   ibid. 12:4

WHAT EVIDENCE MAY BE USED IN DATING BIBLICAL EVENTS?

1. The Bible's historical record

For those who believe that the Bible is the word of G-d or inspired by Him, all its historical details are accepted as true. No other verification is necessary. It is possible to trace the chronological sequence of events and arrive at a relative series of dates for many of the Biblical events and personalities.

This is the approach taken by **Seder Olam**, which meticulously outlines the Bible's timeline and then, where events are quite obviously out of sequence, tries to present an explanation, based on Talmudic and Midrashic sources.

Example: By observing the encampments of the Israelites in the desert, it is clear that Miriam's punishment[4] occurred in the same place as the rebellion of Korach[5], **yet the sin of the spies[6], which happened later, is placed between them.** In his commentary, Rashi states that the Torah wished to compare Miriam, who spoke badly about Moses, with the spies who spoke badly against the land of Israel, so the sin of the spies was taken out of its chronological sequence.

Non-Orthodox scholars do not accept the accuracy of the Biblical chronology. The Bible credits the first ten generations of civilisation with enormous longevity, in some cases over 900 hundred years! They argue that no scientific evidence exists to suggest human beings ever lived for such long periods.

2. Archeological evidence

Until the twentieth century, there was no external method of verifying Biblical narratives. One either believed them to be true or chose not to believe them. Personalities such as Abraham and Moses were seen by 'non-believers' to be mythical folk-heroes who personified praiseworthy characteristics rather than being actual historical figures.

In the last hundred years, however, archeological excavations in the Middle East have certainly verified the general historical reliability of the Bible. Excavations on the southern bank of the River Euphrates have discovered a city called **Mari** containing a place in which were found a collection of cuneiform tablets dating to the Biblical period. It mentions **Haran** (the city to which Abraham and his family moved[7]) as an important political centre, indicating the accuracy of the Biblical geographical record.

---

4   Numbers 12
5   ibid. 16
6   ibid. 13
7   Genesis 11:29

Many personalities named in the tablets have similar names to people mentioned in the Bible. This again indicates contemporary accuracy, since name popularity changes over the generations. In the late 1960's, a stele was discovered in Jordan indicating a person called Bila'am son of Be'or as a fellow well-known for dispensing advice concerning fertility, a description that is consistent with the Bible's description of Bila'am.

The word Habiru or Apiru appears in over 200 of the Ancient Near Eastern texts discovered by archeologists. It usually refers to a class (or type) of people rather than an ethnic race. They are consistently portrayed as 'outsiders' and 'different' to other people. The Biblical identification of the Hebrews as the sole believers in monotheism would be consistent with these archeological findings.

Historians have noted the similarity of the Biblical covenants to the ancient Hittite covenants discovered in archeological findings of ancient texts. In Hittite 'suzerainty' treaties, one party is usually much more powerful than the other and agrees to provide protection and prosperity in return for compliance with a set of laws and sometimes with a tribute to be paid.

Typically, the texts would follow a four-fold pattern:
- *the circumstances* which led up to the covenant being made
- *the rules* and conditions of the covenant
- a list of *witnesses* present at the signing of the covenant
- a series of *blessings and curses* intended to encourage compliance

The covenant at Mount Sinai follows a very similar pattern:
- circumstances:- the exodus from Egypt
- rules:-   the ten commandments/social laws
- witnesses:-the elders (at the end of Deuteronomy, heaven and earth!)
- blessings/curses:- in numerous places in the Torah

Besides the search for documents, archeologists also attempted to find evidence for the existence of cities and buildings mentioned in the Bible. In the 1930's, archeologists thought they had discovered ancient Jericho when remains of a Canaanite city were discovered in that region with evidence of having been destroyed by fire and earthquake. But further research in the 1950's suggested that the city was destroyed a thousand years before the Joshua story. Even this, however, is not conclusive and the debate continues.

Archeological excavations, however, have uncovered the Canaanite city of Hazor, destroyed by Joshua[8]. They found the ruins of a city that clearly came to a sudden and violent end in the same time period as that suggested by the Bible, adding credibility to the Biblical account.

---

8   see Joshua 11

Conclusion

At best, archeological evidence can only give hints rather than solid evidence. Virtually every archeological discovery could be interpreted by believers in the Bible to support the Biblical narrative.

Others would see archeological findings as casting doubt or uncertainty over Biblical records. Why isn't Moses, the greatest Biblical character of all, mentioned in any archeological finding of any other nation? Outside the Bible, there is no evidence that he ever existed.

Alternatively, no archeological finding has ever categorically disproved the truth of any Biblical story.

DATING THE

PRINCIPAL EVENTS

IN THE BIBLE

Creation

Even though it is almost universally accepted scientifically that *the universe is billions of years old*, the chronology of the Bible would suggest it is less than 6000 years old. Seder Olam deflects this scientific challenge to the Biblical chronology by claiming that *the Biblical chronology begins with the creation of Adam on day six*, not from day one. Between day one and day six there may well have been billions of years. Modern scholars have also noted that, as yet, *no fossil remains of human beings have been found that are more than 6000 years old!*

Non-Jewish scholars suggest that the Creation narrative is not to be understood literally, but as a moral tale depicting the sources of good and evil. Its purpose is to introduce the Biblical perspective on the role of humanity and not to provide a historical source for the universe.

The Flood

By counting the years in the genealogy tables in the early chapters of Genesis, the flood is dated at 1656 years from creation, corresponding to 2104 BCE. Biberfeld notes that this date is remarkably close to the dates of flood stories from other ancient religions, most notably the Babylonian Epic of Gilgamesh and the commencement of the Indian Silver Age, which also followed a "great deluge". He goes on to show that almost every ancient religion and mythology makes reference to a flood story. The similarity of dates certainly gives credibility to the point of view that the flood was a historical event, as do the findings of more recent archaeological excavations at the Biblical Mount Ararat in Turkey, the supposed resting place of the Ark.

Abraham

The story of Abraham begins a more historical account of G-d's relationship with humanity. Archeologists have failed to uncover any external verification for the existence of Abraham outside the Bible. The early twentieth century archeologist, W. Albright, however, describes findings depicting nomadic tradesmen who were common in the time period that the Bible accords to Abraham. They lived in tents rather than permanent dwellings and were constantly moving from place to place buying and selling their wares. He surmises that Abraham (and also Isaac and Jacob) were nomadic tradesmen and when serious famine wiped out all trading opportunities, Jacob and his family moved to Egypt.

Modern scholars have pointed out that, by using the Biblical genealogical tables, the birth of Abraham, traditionally identified as the first Jew, is 1948 years from the creation, corresponding to 1812 BCE. It is a remarkable coincidence that the modern state of Israel attained political independence in 1948. This coincidence of dates, whilst not evidence in itself, is highly suggestive.

The Exodus from Egypt

By continuing the Bible's chronology, Seder Olam dates the Exodus from Egypt at *500 years from the birth of Abraham.* The Talmudic debate concludes that the "400 years of exile" prophesized to Abraham at the covenant between the parts[9] began from the birth of Isaac when Abraham (as the Torah states) was 100 years old. This *dates the Exodus at 2448 from the creation, corresponding to 1312 BCE.*

No archeological evidence has yet been uncovered to corroborate the Exodus narrative. Many scholars, noting the similarities of the Sinai covenant (forty days after the Exodus) to the Mesopotamian Code of Hammurabi and other Ancient Near Eastern treaties, have assumed that they were of a similar time period, which would date the Exodus about 500-750 years earlier than the Bible's date.

Biberfeld, however, notes that archaeological excavations of ancient Egypt have discovered *a gap in the Egyptian dynastic order at approximately the same time as the Biblical account of the Exodus.* The archaeological evidence suggests some enormous disaster which destroyed both the Egyptian economy and the military machine. This is certainly consistent with the narrative of the ten plagues and the destruction of the Egyptian army in the Red Sea, as related at the beginning of Exodus.

King David

David's life is described in **Samuel** and **I Chronicles**. He is identified as being from the tribe of **Judah** and, consequently, a potential "rightful" king of Israel according to the blessing of Jacob at the end of Genesis. Following the chronology of the Bible, 40 years after leaving Egypt (1312 BCE), *Israel entered the Promised Land (1272 BCE) and Joshua led them for a further 28 years (1244 BCE).* The period of **Judges**, according to the tables in Seder Olam, *lasted 316 years (928 BCE)* and the rule of *Eli 40 years (888 BCE).*

Samuel judged the people for *13 years (875 BCE)* and David became king the following year at the age of 30. He reigned for 40 years, making the years of his reign *874-834 BCE.*

Alternatively, working backwards from the *destruction of the Second Temple (70 CE)* an identical time scale emerges. The Babylonian Talmud (Bava Bathra) states that the *Second Temple stood for 420 years* thus it was *built in 350 BCE.* Now Jeremiah prophesized that between the destruction of the First Temple and building of the Second Temple *the exile would last 70 years.* This would lead to the *First Temple being destroyed in 420 BCE.*

---

9   see Genesis 11

The same Talmudic source states that the *First Temple stood for 410 years*, thus it was *built in 830 BCE*. The Talmud states *King Solomon* was only 16 when he built the Temple, four years after becoming king, so he *became king in 834 BCE*.

This coincided with the death of his father, King David who, according to the Bible, was 70 when he died. King David was born, therefore, in 904 BCE identical to the above calculation. Either way, *King David is dated, according to Jewish chronology, at the tenth century BCE.*

Biberfeld suggests that excavations of ancient Jerusalem are consistent with the Biblical account of it becoming Israel's capital during David's reign.

Isaiah

The book of Isaiah states that he lived thought *the reigns of four kings of Judah: Uzziah, Yotham, Achaz and Hezekiah.* Seder Olam, by comparing chronological tables of the kings of Judea as found in the books of Kings, dates this period as *approximately 660-560 BCE.* Biberfeld points out that this time period coincides with archaeological datings of the **Assyrian Empire** at approximately the same time. Mediaeval scholars deduce from statements in some of his earlier prophecies that Isaiah witnessed the Assyrian conquest of the ten northern tribes.

Students of Form Criticism suggest that **the literary style of the first 39 chapters of Isaiah is very different to the style of Chapters 40-66.** They therefore suggest that there were two (or more) Isaiahs living at different time periods whose prophecies were later edited into one book. Orthodox scholars have never agreed with this theory and there is no actual historical evidence to support it.

Daniel

In the Talmud Daniel is mentioned as **one of those who went into exile** following the destruction of the First Temple. He is counted as one of the **men of the Great Assembly** convened by Ezra and is believed to have survived into the period of Persian rule. The Medrash on Esther identifies **Hasach** (Esther's chamberlain) as Daniel. When Haman found out that Hasach/Daniel was Jewish, the Medrash continues, he had him assassinated.

Biberfeld points out that although *there is no external historical evidence to corroborate the Talmudic account*, it is known that Jews such as Daniel would have been slaves of the Babylonian court and would have expected to have maintained their positions following the Persian conquest.

The Exiles

There are three different exiles, only the first two of which occur in the Biblical period:

The exile of the Northern Kingdom

The Assyrian conquest of Israel and exile of the ten tribes in mentioned both in the second book of Kings and in Chronicles. It is prophesized by Hosea and by Amos. The chronological tables of Seder Olam date the Assyrian conquest at 555 BCE, which, as pointed out by Biberfeld, corresponds to the archaeological records of the Assyrian empire.

The exile of the Southern Kingdom

The Babylonian conquest of the southern kingdom of Judea and destruction of the First Temple is dated at approximately 420 BCE (see notes on King David for how this date is reached).

Biberfeld analyses archaeological records of the Babylonian period to show how they corroborate this account in quite a lot of detail.

Cuneiform scripts of this period confirm the names of Nebuchadnezzar and Belshazzar as kings of Babylon. They also record Babylon's conquest of Judea. The later details of the Persian conquest of Babylonians as referred to in the later Biblical works has also been corroborated by archaeological findings of Persian records.

The Roman exile

Following the Persian conquest of Babylonia (approximately fifty years after Judea's destruction) the Jewish people enjoyed a period of almost complete security and tolerance (apart from Haman's brief threat during the reign of Achashverosh). The Persians permitted the rebuilding of the Temple and the partial resettlement of the land of Israel, although at no time did the majority of Jews ever return to Israel.

Judea remained a Persian province until the rise of the Greeks. At first this period of tranquility continued. Alexander the Great (the first emperor of Greece) allowed full religious freedom. The Talmud records the Jews' gratitude for this by naming their sons Alexander. This custom continues to the present day. Following Alexander's death and the division of the empire (see notes on the Maccabeean Revolt) things changed.

The later Greek leaders attempted to make the Jews forsake their religion and adopt the culture of Hellenism. Despite the brief respite following the victories of the Maccabees, this pressure to assimilate continued throughout the remainder of the Greek period.

Biberfeld draws attention to the many records from Ancient Greece that highlight their zeal for Hellenization and their ruthless intolerance of other cultures. These records, he concludes, are consistent with the Talmudic account of the Greek period.

The coming of Rome at first alleviated the Jews' problems. The events of this period are recorded both in the Talmud and in the writings of Josephus Flavius. He records that the Romans initially tolerated the Jewish religion, providing the Jews remained obedient to Roman law and diligent in their payment of Roman taxes. Unfortunately, corrupt procurators demanded extortionate taxes and, despite Rabbinic disapproval, this sparked off a revolt against Rome.

In the ensuing war, the Jews were completely annihilated, Jerusalem was destroyed and the Second Temple was burnt to the ground. Josephus's dating of the destruction of the Second Temple in 70 CE has been largely accepted by historians, although some claim that it happened in 68 CE. This date is also recorded in early Christian writings.

The Maccabeean Revolt

It is recorded in the histories of Ancient Greece that, following the death of Alexander the Great, there was no leader who could command the authority to rule the whole Greek empire. It therefore divided into separate principalities which eventually became different kingdoms. The Ptolemaist governed the African part of the empire and the Seleucids governed the Asian part. Judea's geographical situation was very important for the major trading routes linking Central Asia to Africa passed through it. Also, Judea was the only land route linking Africa to Europe. The Ptolemaists and Seleucids therefore fought for control of Judea throughout the third century BCE.

These wars are also referred to in the Talmud. It states that the Ptolemaists were far more tolerant than the Seleucids and that the Jews would assist the Ptolemaists in their struggle. By 200 BCE, however, the Seleucids succeeded in taking permanent control of Judea. Their leaders were particularly zealous to Hellenize their non-Greek subjects. This ruthlessness reached its peak with the accession of Antiochus IV (Epiphanes). Seder Olam dates the beginning of the Maccabbeean revolt against Antiochus at 167 BCE, which approximates reasonably accurately with the Ancient Greek records of the Seleucid period.

The book of Maccabees (which is part of the Apocrypha) records that three years after the revolt began, the Temple was liberated and rededicated. Despite their initial success, however, the Maccabees were unable to remove Seleucid rule from Judea. They did succeed, however, in restoring religious autonomy for the Jews, who were now free to worship in the Temple again. The festival of Chanukah commemorates these events. It is viewed as a celebration, not of a military victory (for victory ultimately was not achieved) but as a restoration of religious liberty.

DOES HISTORICAL ACCURACY REALLY MATTER?

POINTS IN FAVOUR:

1) It points to the accuracy/reliability of the Bible:
It is easier to respect the authors of the books if all their words are known to be accurate. If someone would make a mistake on the history, maybe their other conclusions are also questionable. Knowing the Bible is historically accurate, therefore, allows the student to trust the other material as well.

2) It adds to the store of historical scholarship:
If the Bible's accuracy is assured, other historical and archaeological researchers can rely on its findings to assist them in properly understanding their own discoveries.

3) It helps to get a wider picture of world history:
Just as the discovery of all the ancient civilisations enriches our store of knowledge, so does a thorough study of the historical narratives of the Bible help us to understand what life was really like in the Middle East thousands of years ago.

4) Knowing when events happen sometimes helps to understand why they happen:
When one understands the wider historical context of an event, it becomes much more understandable. The book of Esther reads like a fairy tale, but if it is understood in the context of the Babylonian/Persian exile it becomes a much more significant story. The Talmud states that Achashverosh's feast at the beginning of Esther was a replica of Belshazzar's feast as recorded in Daniel. Both were mistaken celebrations of the failure of Jeremiah's prophecy (that the exile would end in 70 years) to come true. In this light, the rise of Haman as a Divine punishment for Jewish participation in this feast becomes understandable.

Similarly, the book of Jonah becomes more understandable in its historical context. The Talmud reminds us that Jonah had also appeared in the book of Kings where he warned the northern kingdom of Israel that unless they repented they faced conquest and exile at the hands of the Assyrians. When Jonah was then told to go to Nineveh, the capital of Assyria, it is easier to understand why he did not want to go.

5) It is important to know the source of the laws:
In Jewish law, it is very important to distinguish between Torah laws and later laws enacted by the leaders of each generation. If the Torah's historical claim is accepted, then this clarifies which laws go back to the beginning of the Jewish people and which came later. Later laws may have been decreed for certain circumstances which may no longer apply. Torah laws, however, are intended to be for all time and can never be changed.

POINTS AGAINST:

1) The Bible is not a history book:

Even though the Bible contains a lot of historical narratives, its main purpose is to instruct and provide advice on how to live one's life and become a better person. Stories are only included in the Bible for the sake of their message.

The story of **Korach** in Numbers, for example, teaches of the dangers of jealousy. The envy of one man for the honour accorded to another led to the death of himself and 250 of his followers. In terms of learning the lesson of the story, it does not make any difference when Korach lived.

Similarly, in the episode of **King Saul's failure to destroy Amalek** in I Samuel, many would say that it is more important to understand the dangers of allowing evil to prosper than in knowing in what century the event took place.

There are different opinions about when **Job** lived, or even if he lived at all. Ultimately, however, the book's message about how to cope with tragedy is probably a far more worthwhile study than an analysis of its historical context.

2) There is a vast amount of non-historical material in the Bible:

Large sections of the Bible have no historical importance at all. The book of Psalms will be a source of consolation and inspiration regardless of when it was written. Similarly, the wisdom tracts of Proverbs and Ecclesiastes are not enhanced at all by knowing from which time period they emerged. With most of the prophecies of the Later Prophets, although written in response to the sins of their own generation, their messages are relevant to all generations.

3) Myth provides an alternative truth to history:
(See notes on "Myth" in the section on Form Criticism)

Some scholars would claim that stories such as the **Flood** and the **Tower of Babel** never actually occurred. They were included in the Bible, not because of the truth of the events, but because of the truth of the message in the story. Some would like to understand **Job** in this way as well.

Conclusion:

Each student must compare the two points of view and come to a conclusion of their own based upon the evidence brought in their essay.

PRINCIPAL DATES FROM THE BIBLICAL PERIOD

According to the calculations of Midrash Seder Olam Rabbah

Jewish Year	Common Year	Event
1	3760 BCE	Creation of Adam
1656	2104 BCE	Flood
1948	1812 BCE	Birth of Abraham
2448	1312 BCE	Exodus from Egypt/Ten Commandments
2488	1272 BCE	Israelites enter the Land
2516	1244 BCE	Death of Joshua/Judges period begins
2832	928 BCE	Eli HaKohen – the last Judge
2872	888 BCE	Death of Eli/Samuel becomes leader
2886	874 BCE	David becomes king
2926	834 BCE	Death of David/Solomon becomes king
2930	830 BCE	First Temple built
3340	420 BCE	First Temple destroyed/Babylonian exile
3410	350 BCE	Second Temple built
3820	70 CE	Second Temple destroyed/Roman exile

FORM CRITICISM

IDENTIFYING DIFFERENT TYPES OF LITERATURE FOUND IN JEWISH SCRIPTURES AND UNDERSTANDING THEIR RESPECTIVE PURPOSES:

MYTH

HISTORY

PROPHECY

POETRY

LAW

WISDOM

LITURGY

1. **What is Form Criticism?**

2. **How might it apply to Tenach?**

3. **Why did Bible scholars think the Torah had more than one author?**

4. **Why did Bible scholars think Judaism was a combination of more than one religion?**

5. **How might Torah scholars use Form Criticism?**

1. What is Form Criticism?

Form Criticism is the name given to a method of *analysing Biblical texts*.

It involves *comparing the different literary styles* found in the Bible.

We deal with different types of literature all the time and it is very important to *identify the form correctly.*

For example, a magazine may contain factual stories, fiction and advertisements. We automatically *criticise* the piece we are reading in order to *identify it and interpret it* appropriately.

2. How might it apply to Tenach?

The Bible is just the same. It contains a whole variety of different literary forms and our task is to recognize them so that we can interpret them correctly.

Form Criticism encourages the student of the Bible to *ask two questions:*

1. What kind of form is this narrative?

2. How is it to be interpreted?

The value of Form Criticism is that *it sets interpretive boundaries* around the text. This helps the student to *understand the intention of the author* and *the message of the text.*

The Torah, for example, contains many different literary styles. Although it reads as one continuous narrative from Genesis to Deuteronomy, it contains historical narratives, prophecies, poetry and laws. Some narratives and laws, such as the Ten Commandments, are duplicated. It is always valid to analyze a written document to find internal clues about its structure, its author, the circumstances of its writing, and the possible number of times it was edited. This is called *literary analysis.*

Here is a modern example of literary analysis:

You receive a typewritten letter from your grandmother. She suddenly changes subject in the middle of the letter. Why? Did the phone ring and, when she returned, a new thought occurred to her? Or did your grandfather say something that set her off on a different subject? Or did your grandfather finish off the letter for her?

Literary analysis looks for the reason why style changes in the document being studied.

3. Why did Bible scholars think the Torah had more than one author?

Eighteenth and nineteenth century (mostly non-Jewish and/or non-religious) scholars such as Hermann Gunkel believed that the existence of different styles of literature within the same book indicated different authors working in different time periods or possibly that the book in question was a composite of different earlier works that had been put together to form a new work.

It has been suggested, for example, that since the literary form of Deuteronomy is different to the other four books of the Torah, it *was probably written at a later time* by different scholars and then added to the Torah. Orthodox Judaism would not accept this conclusion. It would acknowledge, however, that there is significance to the different literary forms. Rabbinic scholars also noticed the different style of Deuteronomy.

They suggest that the entire book represents *the 'farewell address' of Moses* before his death and is therefore written from Moses' perspective ("And G-d said to me...") rather than from G-d's perspective ("And G-d said to Moses...")[10] as is found in Exodus, Leviticus and Numbers.

4. Why did Bible scholars think Judaism was a combination of more than one religion?

According to Orthodox tradition, the Torah was written down by Moses. Form Criticism scholars challenged this assertion. *What about those passages of the Torah that describe Moses' death and burial?* How could he have written them? Similarly, Joshua is accredited authorship of his book by the Talmud, yet his death is recorded in the final chapter!

1500 years before the first form criticism studies, the Talmud had already asked this question.[11] Most scholars conclude that *Joshua completed the Torah* and Othniel ben Kenaz (the first Judge) completed the book of Joshua. Even today, if an author dies after completing the bulk of a work and someone else finishes off the final chapter and adds a few concluding comments about the death of the author, we have no problem attributing the whole work to the original author.

Bible critics were also troubled by the use of a *different name of G-d* in Genesis 2 to that which appears in Genesis 1. They suggested that these two chapters represent two different creation stories that were later woven into one. This idea is supported by the twentieth century (non-religious) Jewish writer Max I. Dimont in his book *Jews, G-d and History*. He suggests *there were two 'Israelite' groupings*, one in Cana'an and one that were slaves that escaped from Egypt. When the slaves conquered Cana'an and made it their own, they combined their creation story with the one of the Cana'anites.

Orthodox scholars reject this answer and explain that the Talmud discusses different names of G-d found in the Bible and identifies *each name as representing a different*

---

10   see Commentary to Deuteronomy (Introduction) by Ramban [Nachmanides] (1194-1270) acknowledged leader of Spanish Jewry in his generation

11   TB Bava Bathra 15a

attribute of G-d. Genesis 1 describes what G-d created and so uses the name which depicts G-d's power and strength (Elokim). Genesis 2, however, describes how G-d accomplished the creation, everything being done with love and compassion for His creation, and uses a name which depicts G-d's mercy (the tetragrammaton).[12]

Non-Jewish scholars such as Heinrich Ewald acknowledged that the Bible's historical narratives were based on factual events but suggested that they had been *exaggerated and romanticised* over the generations of oral transmission so that, by the time they were written down, the characters' personalities appeared far more righteous or more wicked than they actually were.

It is certainly true that evidence exists for the romanticisation of characters from other ancient sources. Most scholars accept today that King Arthur did exist, but it is generally accepted that there is little factual basis for many of the stories told about him. The same could be said for Robin Hood and the Swiss mediaeval hero William Tell. *There is no Biblical evidence to support Ewald's suggestion,* however, and Orthodox scholars would point out that many stories told about Jewish leaders have been proven to be accurate.

5. How might Torah scholars use Form Criticism?
Even though most Orthodox scholars totally reject Form Criticism, many agree that *different literary styles indicate the necessity for a different approach to the study of the respective texts.* Form criticism would not be used to identify authorship, since the Talmud[13] clearly identified the authors of each Biblical work (see Origin of Tenach in Judaism AS for details). Rather, different literary styles would be seen as indicating different emphases and highlighting different moral or ethical lessons, as will be explained.

Conclusion

Form Criticism will *attempt to classify Biblical works,* for example, as 'myth', 'historical narrative', 'poetry' or 'law'. It will also attempt to *understand the intention of the author.* Was a poem written to be used for liturgical purposes (i.e. as a prayer)? Did a historical narrative convey a particular message? All this is intended to increase our understanding of why the Bible was written and what its original purpose was.

---

12   Genesis Rabba 12:15; Exodus Rabba 30:13; Pesikta Rabasi 40 – quoted by Rashi: Genesis 1:1

13   TB Bava Bathra 14b-15a

MYTH

NOT EVERY NARRATIVE THAT APPEARS IN THE BIBLE IS HISTORICALLY TRUE. MAIMONIDES WRITES THAT THE BIBLE OCCASIONALLY USES PARABLES AS EDUCATIONAL TOOLS. MESSAGES ARE PRESENTED IN THE FORM OF A STORY IN SUCH A WAY THAT PEOPLE OF ALL AGES AND LEVELS OF UNDERSTANDING CAN ABSORB DIFFERENT ASPECTS OF THE MESSAGE, EACH ACCORDING TO HIS ABILITIES.

Nathan's rebuke of King David

An example of myth is found in the second book of Samuel. The prophet Nathan was instructed to rebuke King David following his taking of Bathsheba as a wife.

> There were two men in one city, one rich and one poor. The rich man had very many flocks and herds. But the poor man had nothing save one little lamb which he had bought and reared... And there came a traveler to the rich man and he declined to take of his own flock... for the guest... but he took the poor man's lamb and prepared it for [the traveller][14]

Nathan compared the rich man to David, who had taken the wife of another when he already had many of his own. On a simple level the parable was a way for Nathan to give David a rebuke that he would understand. On a deeper level, the Talmud compares the traveler to the evil inclination who entices the ordinary person (the rich man) to sin.[15]

The trees pick a leader

Another example is Yotham's warning parable in the book of Judges:

> When it was told to Yotham, he went and stood on the top of Mt Gerizim, and cried aloud and said to them: Listen to me, lords of Shechem, so that G-d may listen to you. The trees once went out to anoint a king over themselves. They said to the olive tree: reign over us. But the olive tree answered:, Shall I stop producing my rich oil by which G-d and men are honored to sway over the trees?' Then the trees said to the fig tree: You come and reign over us. But the fig tree answered them: Shall I stop producing my sweetness and my delicious fruit to sway over the trees? Then the trees said to the vine: You come and reign over us. But the vine said to them: Shall I stop producing my wine that causes G-d and man to rejoice to sway over the trees?' Then all the trees said to the bramble: You come and reign over us. And the bramble said to the trees: If in good faith you are anointing me king over you, then come and take refuge in my shade; but if not, let fire come out of the bramble and devour the cedars of Lebanon.[16]

Following Gideon's victory over the Midianites, the people wished to appoint him as their king. Yotham wanted to warn the people about the dangers of appointing a king. The most popular interpretation of this parable is that the trees refer to the Judges who had specific tasks which benefited Israel, the bramble representing the wicked Abimelech who became a Judge by murdering the sons of Gideon and ruling in their place.

The suffering of the righteous

Often, a subject that is difficult to understand will be made more comprehensible by the use of a parable. One of the deepest of religious studies concerns attempting to understand why it is, if there really is a G-d, that righteous people suffer and wicked people prosper. Many scholars view the book of Job as a parable which grapples with this problem.

---

14   II Samuel 12:2-4
15   see TB Sukkah 52b
16   Judges 9:7-15

When understood on this level, it can be said that all parables are true, in that they present a message that is true, even if the story itself may never have actually happened. Rabbeinu Bachya[17] illustrates the importance of parables with a parable!

> A man lost a valuable diamond in a very dark place. He knew the diamond was there but he could not see it. By lighting a small candle, which in itself is worth very little indeed, he was able to find his precious jewel.

A virtually worthless piece of wax and thread assumes great importance when it allows us to find something of immense value. Similarly, many of the concepts found in the Bible are difficult to grasp. A simple story may have very little worth in itself, but when used to illustrate or simplify a complicated idea, just like the worthless candle, it becomes very important.

What is fact? What is myth? Does it matter?

There is a wide difference of opinion concerning whether or not certain Biblical narratives are fact or myth. Both mythological and historical narratives serve the purpose of promoting ethical or moral ideas. Where a true story exists that serves this purpose, it would not be necessary to compose a myth.

There are numerous examples of miraculous occurrences in the Bible. Whilst traditionally all these stories are understood as historical events, modern scholars might understand some of these narratives as myths which promote moral or ethical teachings:

Creation
Virtually all Orthodox Jewish scholars consider the Creation and Garden of Eden narratives to be historical. Maimonides, however, suggests that the reason that these events are included in the Bible is for the purpose of teaching important messages about the nature of humanity and its responsibility for preserving G-d's creation. It is not to be read as a factual account of how the world was created, a subject beyond the grasp of human intelligence.

Balaam
Bala'am's talking donkey[18] teaches an important lesson concerning man's frailty. The arrogant Midianite sorcerer Bala'am claimed to be able to influence G-d to curse Israel. Whilst on his way to impose this curse, his donkey miraculously began to speak. In the ensuing argument between Bala'am and the donkey, the donkey won!

---

17   Bachya Ibn Pakuda. 11th century Spanish philosopher.

18   Numbers 22

Far from influencing G-d, Bala'am could not even influence his own donkey! The arrogance of Bala'am and his abject failure teach the lesson of humility in dealing with those we consider less able than ourselves, regardless of whether or not the donkey actually talked.

1000 wives

King Solomon's marriage to 1000 wives[19] is difficult to comprehend rationally. How could one man be a husband to so many women? Yet the Talmud's main concern is to present a different message of humility. Despite being 'wiser than all men', King Solomon chose to ignore the Torah's advice not to take too many wives lest they turn away his heart. He did not believe he could be corrupted. This particular lesson of humility, that even a great scholar must acknowledge that there are things he does not understand, is more important than the number of wives King Solomon took.

Right over might

The miraculous defeat of Jericho[20] by Joshua would promote a belief in the superiority of 'right' over 'might'. The city walls did not fall down because of the greater military ability of the Israelites, but because of the wickedness of the Cana'anites.

David's victory of Goliath[21] promotes a similar message. The prophet emphasises the strength of Goliath and the fact that what David did was not, in itself, an explanation of his success. It was David's righteousness that prompted G-d to perform a miracle for him rather than his ability with a slingshot.

The book of Jonah promotes the value of sincere repentance and provides a perspective on human suffering and the nature of free will, regardless of whether or not Jonah was actually swallowed by a big fish. Similarly, the messianic visions of Daniel inspire hope for a better future regardless of whether or not those dreams had any factual significance.

---

19   I Kings 11

20   Joshua 6

21   I Samuel 17

HISTORY

HISTORICAL NARRATIVE IS BY FAR THE LARGEST COMPONENT OF THE BIBLE. DESPITE THIS FACT, ENORMOUS QUANTITIES OF HISTORICAL INFORMATION, RELEVANT TO THIS TIME PERIOD, ARE COMPLETELY OMITTED. EVEN THOUGH THIS IS ALSO TRUE OF THE HISTORICAL RECORDS OF OTHER ANCIENT CIVILISATIONS, BIBERFELD POINTS OUT A VERY IMPORTANT DIFFERENCE BETWEEN THE PURPOSE OF HISTORICAL NARRATIVES IN THE BIBLE AND THEIR PURPOSE IN OTHER ANCIENT CIVILISATIONS.

What do we use history for?

Ancient civilisations tended to record only their victories and omitted their defeats. They are full of praise for their leaders, perfect specimens (in some cases gods) who can do no wrong. The Bible on the other hand is replete with references to Israel's and her leaders' sins. The entire book of Judges, for example, is an apparently merciless castigation of Israel's unfaithfulness to G-d. Similarly, in the Torah, the journeys through the wilderness are replete with references to the Israelites' sinfulness.

The Bible also takes great pains to emphasise that even Israel's greatest leaders are but mortal human beings who are capable of error and sin. Moses' parentage and lineage is carefully noted, so that no future generation will accord him the status of a deity. His sin of striking the rock led to his punishment of being prohibited entry into the Promised Land. King David is reprimanded on a number of occasions for unseemly conduct and is not permitted to build the Temple.

Orthodox scholars would give two explanations for this difference to the historical records of ancient civilisations. This would clarify, according to traditional opinion, the role of historical material in the Bible:

The Bible emphasises the greatness of G-d not the greatness of Israel.

The Bible details Israel's sins and the consequent punishments they received. It also demonstrates that, when Israel repents and returns to the righteous path, all her enemies are vanquished and she enjoys peace and tranquility. The book of Judges traces a pattern that begins in peace and tranquility. This 'easy life' leads to laxness in religious observance, which in turn leads to the success of an enemy in plundering and occupying their land. A leader then arises, such as Deborah or Gideon who will induce the people to repent and renew their commitment to the Torah, following which there is a great military victory, enemies are vanquished and peace and tranquility is restored. One of the essential purposes of historical narrative, therefore, is to draw attention to this message so that *future generations will learn from and (hopefully) not repeat the mistakes of their ancestors.*

The Bible is a book of instruction not a history book.

Historical narratives are only considered to have importance insomuch as they teach a lesson that is relevant to future generations. The entire episode of Eliezer finding a wife for Isaac[22] is told in minute detail, despite having minimal historical value, yet over 1600 years of history from Cain's murder of Abel until the incident of the Flood is related in a few short sentences.

---

22   Genesis 24

Eliezer's journey teaches many principles about how to approach marriage, as is elucidated by the classical commentaries of Rashi[23] and Ramban[24], and is therefore accorded much space. The degeneration of civilisation has few lessons of lasting worth and so can be dismissed in a few short lines. The 'instruction value' of a historical incident, consequently, will be the determining factor in the emphasis (or even inclusion) of such an event in the Bible rather than its historical significance.

Location
Historical narrative is found in all three sections of the Bible.

In the Torah:
The entire book of Genesis and the first half of Exodus are exclusively historical. *Genesis* explains the emergence of the Jewish people from the creation until the descent to Egypt in the days of Jacob. *Exodus* describes the slavery in Egypt, the redemption, the revelation at Mount Sinai and the sin of the golden calf. The death of Aaron's oldest two sons is told in *Leviticus*. *Numbers* contains the historical record of Israel's travels in the wilderness. *Deuteronomy* recounts much of what happened during the wilderness period and concludes with the death of Moses and accession of Joshua.

In the Prophets:
The book of *Joshua* records Israel's conquest of the land. *Judges* relates many events from the pre-monarchist period. *Samuel* records the periods of Samuel, King Saul and King David. *Kings* opens with the accession of King Solomon and building of the First Temple, the historical peak of Israel's physical powers. It then charts their gradual decline: division into two kingdoms, civil war, *Assyrian exile* of the northern kingdom of Israel, *Babylonian exile* of the southern kingdom of Judea and *destruction of the First Temple*. The later prophets also make reference to many historical events from the period covered by the book of Kings. For example, *Jonah* highlights the repentance of Nineveh and *Jeremiah* describes the days before and immediately after the destruction of the Temple in vivid detail.

In the Writings:
The book of *Ruth* gives further elucidation of the period of the Judges. A number of books contain valuable historical information about the exile period between the two Temples. *Daniel* makes reference to life under Babylonian rule. *Esther* describes life in the Persian exile. *Ezra/Nehemiah* explains the difficulties encountered in the rebuilding of the Temple and partial resettlement of the Promised Land. Finally, *Chronicles* provides a historical panorama of the entire Biblical period.

---

23   Rabbi Shlomo Yitzchaki (1040-1105) French scholar considered the greatest of the mediaeval commentators.

24   see note 1

PROPHECY

THE HEBREW WORD FOR PROPHET IS NAVI, WHICH IS A NOUN FORM OF THE VERB MEVI, WHICH MEANS 'BRING'. A PROPHET, CONSEQUENTLY, IS UNDERSTOOD BY JEWISH TRADITION TO BE ONE WHO BRINGS THE MESSAGE OF G-D TO THE PEOPLE. THE VAST MAJORITY OF BIBLICAL PROPHECIES WERE WARNINGS OF IMPENDING (OR FUTURE) DISASTER UNLESS THE PEOPLE FORSOOK THEIR SINFUL WAYS.

PROPHECY WAS NOT NECESSARILY A PREDICTION OF FUTURE EVENTS. IT COULD ALSO TAKE THE FORM OF A WARNING BASED ON PAST EVENTS. LARGE SECTIONS OF PROPHETS (INCLUDING VIRTUALLY ALL OF JUDGES, SAMUEL AND KINGS) SEEM TO BE HISTORICAL NARRATIVES WITHOUT ANY PROPHETIC MESSAGE. THE MESSAGE, HOWEVER, IS IN THE STORY, WHICH IS A WARNING FOR FUTURE GENERATIONS THAT THEY SHOULD NOT STUMBLE INTO THE SAME ERRORS AS THEIR ANCESTORS.

What is Prophecy?

Maimonides[25] defines prophecy as *a message from G-d for the benefit of the people*. Not every future prediction is necessarily a prophecy. G-d's message to Abraham at the 'covenant between the parts'[26] that his descendants would be slaves in Egypt, is not considered a prophecy since it does not contain an instruction to pass this information on to anybody. Similarly, Daniel received no instruction to relay the contents of his messianic visions to the people. They would be understood as words of consolation and inspiration rather than prophecy.

The prophet, thus, is an individual chosen by God, often against his will, to reveal G-d's intentions and plans to the people. As a bearer of divine revelation, he will experience G-d's overwhelming presence and receive the strength to communicate to others what G-d has said, even though this may lead to persecution, suffering, and, in the case of Isaiah, death by assassination. Scholars have identified **four different types of prophecy** in the Tenach:

1) *Mystic trance.* The best example of this is found in the first book of Samuel[27] when the young *Saul encounters a band of prophets* prophesizing. Targum Yonatan describes such bands as disciples of the great prophets of the time. They would immerse themselves in spiritual matters and completely disassociate themselves from the material world. Through this deep contemplation, they would attain a spiritual elevation that enabled a lower level of prophetic understanding.

2) *Seers.* This title is identified with *Samuel* who, according to Talmudic tradition, was the greatest prophet after Moses. Regular prophecy gave general advice to individuals or specific advice to groups, but a Seer could give specific advice to an individual. Redak[28] writes that Seers were only found in the earlier period, before there was a king.

3) *False Prophets.* Only identified in the Tenach in the later period following the division of the kingdoms, they were genuine prophets who misunderstood the messages they received. They were *principally associated with Jeremiah*, whose message they opposed. They advised resistance and rebellion against the Babylonians whereas Jeremiah advised surrender and acceptance of their rule in order to retain their religious freedom and their Temple.

---

25   Guide for the Perplexed II:49

26   Genesis 12

27   I Samuel 10:5-13

28   Commentary to I Samuel 9:9

4) Court Prophets. They advised and were the 'conscience' of the monarch. They are found throughout the Biblical period. *Nathan*[29] rebukes King David for taking Bathsheba as a wife. *Isaiah* warned a number of kings of the folly of their conduct. Many prophets (most famously *Jeremiah*) warned of the destruction of the Temple and impending exile. Another popular theme of the court prophets was their abhorrence of the abuse of animal sacrifices. They were not opposed to the sacrifices themselves, but to the empty practice of a ritual devoid of any moral or ethical force. The sacrifice was to be a dynamic that inspired moral and ethical improvement, not a substitute for it.

Location

Prophecies are found only in the first two sections of the Bible. This is because, according to Talmudic tradition, all the books of Writings were communicated through Divine Inspiration which is a level lower than prophecy

In the Torah:

Major prophecies are found at the end of Leviticus and near the end of Deuteronomy. They tell of the blessings and curses that will befall the Jewish people as a consequence of their observance (or failure to observe) the commandments of the Torah. The later chapters of Deuteronomy are also believed to contain allusions to the messianic era, although their precise meaning is difficult to decipher.

> And it shall be when all these things have come upon you, the blessing and the curse, which I have put before you; and you will reflect in your hearts when you [dwell] among the nations where G-d will have exiled you. Then you will return to the Lord your G-d and you will hear [obey] His voice according to all which I have commanded you today... G-d will then return your remnant... [and] gather you from among the nations where He scattered you... and He will bring you back... to the land that your ancestors possessed and you shall posses it...[30]

In the Prophets:

All the books of this section are naturally considered to be prophetic works. The *Early Prophets* are all examples of prophetic works with no future prediction, but with a warning for the future contained in their narratives. The *Later Prophets* are the more traditionally known prophetic works. (see see **Content of Tenach** in **Judaism AS** for specific examples of each prophecy).

In the Writings:

As previously, mentioned, the books of the Writings are considered to be written on a spiritual level lower than that of the Prophets, the level of Divine Inspiration. None of these books, consequently, are considered to be prophetic works.

---

29   II Samuel 12
30   Deuteronomy 30:1-5

The importance of prophecy

The Talmud states that one of the punishments that accompanied the destruction of the First Temple was that prophecy ceased. This cessation of prophecy, far more than even the destruction of the Temple, was seen as the catastrophe that brought the Biblical period to an end.

The Biblical period was one in which Israel, as it were, had a direct 'hot-line' to G-d. It is recorded that, before going into battle against the Philistines, King Saul contacted the spirit of the recently deceased prophet Samuel to ask if he would be victorious in battle. When Samuel asked why Saul had disturbed him, the king replied:

> ... G-d has turned away from me and has not answered me any more, neither through prophets nor through dreams...[31]

From here, it was deduced that, before any major undertaking, a prophet's advice was always sought. With the loss of prophecy, a great security was removed from the people. It had provided a certainty (for those who wished to know) exactly what was the will of G-d. It was also a means for G-d to communicate with His people when the need arose. Prophecy was, therefore, a very important aspect of life in the Biblical period.

Ever since then, Jews have been left the words of the prophets to study. Scholars in each generation have studied and interpreted their words as warnings and exhortations for their own times. Messianic fervor has often been excited by the 'new' interpretation of an obscure prophetic passage. Sections of Ezekiel are considered the principal sources for the study of Kabbalah, Jewish mysticism, which is popular particularly among the Chassidic sects. In every Shabbat and festival morning service, following the reading of the Torah portion of the week or festival, a related section of the prophets is also read. All this ensures that the relevance of the prophetic works is not forgotten.

---

31   I Samuel 28:15

POETRY

IN LITERATURE GENERALLY, NARRATIVE PROSE (BE IT HISTORICAL OR MYTHICAL) WILL PRESENT AN APPEAL TO A PERSON'S INTELLECT. POETRY, BY WAY OF CONTRAST, WILL PRESENT AN APPEAL TO A PERSON'S EMOTIONS. WHERE PROSE AND POETRY ARE COMBINED IN THE SAME NARRATIVE, IT COULD BE UNDERSTOOD AS AN INITIAL EFFORT TO EXPLAIN AND CLARIFY AN ISSUE FOLLOWED BY AN ATTEMPT CHARGE A PERSON'S EMOTIONS, BE IT WITH ANGER, RELIEF, JOY, DESPAIR, LOVE OR PITY. THERE ARE A NUMBER OF POETIC COMPOSITIONS IN THE BIBLE, MANY OF WHICH COMPLEMENT A PROSE NARRATIVE AND REPRESENT ITS EPITAPH.

One of the outstanding features of the Jewish Scriptures is the beauty of its poetry, which is not restricted to the obvious poetic compositions. The words of the prophets are frequently expressed poetically, especially Isaiah and Jeremiah. Job, even though classified as wisdom literature, also contains some extremely moving poetic sections.

Poetry in the Torah

The Song at the Red Sea[32]
Following Israel's miraculous escape following the splitting of the sea to let them pass and the immediate destruction of the Egyptian army as the waters returned, the Israelites expressed their joy and relief in a song of praise to G-d. Its inclusion in the Biblical narrative serves to provide the reader with an emotional charge as he attempts to understand the mood of the people following their sudden and complete redemption. The song is recited privately by Orthodox Jews every morning in the preliminary morning service. It is also recited publicly from the Torah scroll on the seventh day of Pesach, the anniversary of the original miracle. The Shulchan Aruch[33] states that every Jew should endeavour to experience great joy during its recital.

Moses farewell song/poem (Ha'azinu)[34]
The entire book of Deuteronomy has been understood as an exhortation to Israel concerning her future conduct. As Moses reaches the end of his life, he finishes with a poem bringing all the ideas of this book together. This poetic rendition, which begins with a summons to the heavens and the earth to be witnesses to the covenant between G-d and Israel, is intended to fill the people with enthusiasm for the fulfillment of the covenant that he has been so painstakingly explaining to them.

Poetry in the Prophets

The song of Deborah[35]
Following a miraculous victory over the Canaanites, which is described in great detail, Deborah sings a song of praise to G-d in which all the factors that led to the victory are highlighted. Many commentaries compare this song with the song of the Red Sea, as it appears to serve a similar purpose. On the Shabbat when the song of the Red Sea is recited from the Torah, the victory and song of Deborah are the Haftarah[36] for that week.

---

32   Exodus 15
33   Definitive code of Jewish Law for all Orthodox Jews composed by Rabbi Yosef Caro (1488-1575)
34   Deuteronomy 32
35   Judges 5
36   The prophetic reading which accompanies and complements the weekly Torah portion

David's lament[37]

When David hears news of Israel's defeat by the Philistines and the deaths of King Saul and Jonathan, he recites a heartrending lament for their death. It begins with the famous elegy: ...how are the mighty fallen and is intended to evoke in the reader the feelings of anguish and sorrow that David felt following this enormous tragedy.

Solomon's prayer[38]

Following the construction and inauguration of the First Temple, King Solomon prayed for Israel's success and continued righteous conduct. The prayer is intended to inspire the people (and the reader) to want to come close to G-d, to follow in His ways and to remain loyal to His commands. Rather than telling them to do all these things (an appeal to their minds) he exhorted them through the stirring words of his prayer, that their emotions should be fired with a desire for righteousness.

Poetry in the Writings

Only in this section are entire books of poetic compositions found. As with all the books of this section, their purpose is to inspire and/or console. The poetic style, therefore, is particularly suited to this section of the Bible.

Psalms

The 150 Psalms cover every possible mood or emotional expression. It is probably the most widely read book of the entire Bible. All emotional occasions have appropriate Psalms that can be recited, be it an act of thanksgiving, a celebration of success or an outpouring of grief. There are Psalms that offer hope for the despairing, others that offer comfort when all has been lost. There are also Psalms of consolation to be recited upon visiting a graveyard. By contrast, other Psalms exult with the sheer joy of life. In synagogues, Psalms are often recited communally at times of peril and danger, or as a prayer on behalf of the sick. Many Orthodox Jews make a point of reciting all the Psalms on a regular basis.

Song of Songs

This book is a poem that identifies the deep and passionate emotions that true love evinces. On a simple level, it can be understood as a celebration of the joy experienced by a young couple about to be married. On this level, it is an emotional defence of marriage as the true framework for the greatest human bond. On a deeper level, it is understood as a description of the bond of love that exists between G-d and Israel, and is intended to be an inspiration for every Jew to accept the love of G-d that is offered them. In many Chasidic and Sephardi communities, it is recited in synagogues every Friday evening before the Shabbat evening service, Shabbat being the time when Jews should most be able to feel the closeness and love of G-d.

---

37   II Samuel 1

38   I Kings 8:22-61

Lamentations

This poem is traditionally believed to have been composed by Jeremiah on the day that the First Temple was destroyed. It is an attempt to capture the mood of shock, despair and utter desolation that was experienced at that time. The book ends however with the prayer that G-d should: cause us to return to You and we shall repent; renew our days as of old.[39] In this light it is both an expression of grief and pain with which victims of persecution have been able to identify throughout the generations and also a harbinger of hope for the future, that suffering is not permanent and consolation is at hand.

The importance of Poetry

In Jewish tradition, The Bible is primarily a work to be studied. The poetic sections therefore provide an essential contrast to the narrative prose. They allow the 'complete person' to identify with the Biblical events and ensure that the Bible is not merely a dry historical or legal tome. The songs of Moses (at the Red Sea) and Deborah are intended to express the joy and exhilaration at the sight of one's enemies being vanquished. David's lament and Lamentations, by contrast, are both attempts to capture the mood of anguish and grief, the one personal, the other communal. Poetry brings Biblical narratives to life and allows the reader to be far more involved in them.

39   Lamentations 5:21

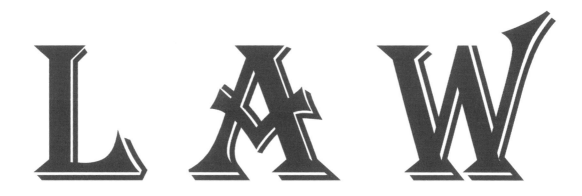

FROM A RELIGIOUS POINT OF VIEW, THE EXPLANATIONS OF THE LAWS ARE THE MOST IMPORTANT SECTIONS OF THE TENACH. THE TENACH WAS ALWAYS INTENDED TO BE A BOOK OF INSTRUCTION AS TO HOW ISRAEL WAS TO FULFILL ITS ROLE AS THE CHOSEN PEOPLE. WITHOUT THE LAWS, THERE COULD NOT BE A JEWISH PEOPLE. THE WORD TORAH IS DERIVED FROM THE HEBREW VERB LEHOROT, WHICH MEANS TO INSTRUCT. ALTHOUGH LEGAL NARRATIVE IS PRIMARILY FOUND IN THE TORAH, THERE ARE REFERENCES TO LAWS ENACTED LATER IN THE BIBLICAL PERIOD IN OTHER SECTIONS OF THE TENACH AS WELL.

Archeological findings have demonstrated that written laws, as a specific literary form, actually existed for many centuries before any part of the Tenach was written down. Some non-Orthodox scholars believe that many of the Biblical laws were based on these ancient laws, but Orthodox scholars do not accept this.

The biblical laws can be classified in different ways. One division is between laws between man and G-d, such as not worshipping idols, offering sacrifices and prayers and observing the festivals and laws between man and his neighbour, such as giving charity, maintaining honest weights and measures and not being a false witness in court.

Another division is between social laws, such as paying compensation on damaging others' property, showing special consideration to orphans and widows and returning lost property and ritual laws, such as the dietary laws, the laws of ritual immersion in a mikvah and the wearing of tzitzit and tefillin.

Yet another division is between those laws believed to be Torah laws, i.e. those given by G-d himself and the Rabbinic laws added later by the leaders of the generations to protect the observance of those laws. For example, the Talmud states that committing adultery is forbidden by Torah law but, following the incident with Bathsheba, King David instituted the law of yichud, which forbids a man and a woman to be secluded alone. They site this as one of the earliest examples of a Rabbinic law.[40]

Location
Although the Torah is the main source of Jewish law, many laws are either introduced or more fully explained in the other sections of the Tenach.

In the Torah
According to Orthodox tradition, the Torah contains 613 commandments, all received from G-d by Moses on Mount Sinai. Although this is a unanimous viewpoint, there is some dispute about which commands are included in the 613. Maimonides, for example, identifies a Torah commandment to pray in the second paragraph of the Shema.[41] Nachmanides disagrees however. He states that it is so obvious that a believer in G-d will pray that there is no need to command it at all. All five books of the Torah contain reference to laws:

Genesis
Only three commands are found here. Adam and Eve are commanded to marry and have children. Abraham is commanded to circumcise all his descendant males when they are eight days old as a sign of the covenant between him and G-d. The prohibition against eating the sinew of the thigh vein is enacted following Jacob's wrestling with the angel, as the sinew of Jacob's thigh vein was wounded in the struggle.

Exodus
The early part of the book, which deals with slavery and redemption from Egypt, makes reference to the Paschal lamb, some of the Pesach laws and to the command to wear tefillin. The major handing down of the law, however, begins approximately half way

---

40   Some aspects of the laws of *Yichud* are also believed to be Torah laws.

41 see Deuteronomy 11 where it says: *and you shall serve Him with all your heart*. Rambam identifies this 'service of the heart' as a command to pray.

through this book with the ten commandments, believed to have been spoken by G-d at Mount Sinai. They are followed by all the social laws (laws governing relationships and possible disputes between people) and the instructions concerning building the Mishkan (the portable sanctuary that hosted the sacrificial service until the First Temple was built).

Leviticus
This book is almost exclusively legalistic. It contains all the laws concerning the daily sacrifice service and the complex details of the laws of ritual purity/impurity which primarily concerned the kohanim. These laws also have contemporary relevance as a basis to the laws of family purity. The laws of kashrut, governing which animals, birds and fish may be eaten are also included in this book. It concludes with the laws concerning the Sabbatical (seventh) year and the Jubilee (fiftieth) year when the land must lie fallow.

Numbers
Many of the laws concerning festival sacrifices are found here. It also contains the laws of the suspect wife, the laws concerning vows, the priestly blessing, originally recited every morning in the Mishkan and Temple and still recited today on festivals. The laws concerning wearing tzitzit and the agricultural tithes that had to be set aside for the Kohen and the Levite are also found here.

Deuteronomy
This book repeats many laws already referred to earlier in the Torah, although scholars have found that each repetition highlights a different aspect of the law not fully covered in earlier books. It repeats the ten commandments but draws attention to fearing parents as well as honouring them and to guarding (i.e. against performing labour on) the Shabbat as well as remembering (i.e. resting on and enjoying) it. It also contains the first two paragraphs of the Shema which repeat the laws of tefillin (but in relation respectively to love of G-d and commitment to observe the commandments) and contain the command to put up a mezzuzah. The book specifically focuses on all the practical laws dealing with living in the land of Israel, such as the agricultural laws, the laws of courts and the establishing of a monarchy.

In the Prophets
All new laws contained in the later sections of the Bible would come under the general category of Rabbinic laws, i.e. laws enacted by leaders of the Jewish people in response to the circumstances of their times. Sometimes, however, the detailed explanations of Torah laws are also found here, especially when the Torah itself only makes brief reference to them.

Joshua
The laws of the cities of refuge, to where an accidental murderer must flee, are detailed at the time Joshua established the cities, following the conquest of the land. These laws are first mentioned briefly in Numbers and Deuteronomy.

Samuel

In Deuteronomy, G-d instructs the people that there will come a time when they will appoint a king. The laws concerning the powers of a king, however, are not listed. Samuel explains these powers in detail as a warning to the people when they prematurely requested that a king be appointed over them.

Jonah

Many of the laws concerning repentance are derived both from the prayer of Jonah in the belly of the fish and from the response of the Ninevites to Jonah's prophecy. Maimonides states that the process of repentance: regret for one's actions; remorse for their consequences; resolution not to repeat the same transgression again; is based on Jonah's prayer. The completion of the penitential process, being in the same situation again and not repeating one's sin, is deduced from G-d's second call to Jonah to go to Nineveh.

In the Writings

Job

Many of the laws of mourning, such as sitting on the floor (or low stools) and offering a meal of consolation are derived from Job's response to his suffering.

Ruth

Many of the conversion laws are derived from the dialogue between Naomi and Ruth, i.e. that a convert must initially be dissuaded not encouraged to convert; and that one converts only for the sake of fulfilling the commandments. From Boaz's actions, there is an example of the Torah law to show particular regard and concern for the convert.

Esther

The closing chapters of this book detail the laws governing the Rabbinic festival of Purim. Some modern scholars have tried to deduce from these laws the rationale for establishing festivals of Rabbinic status in an attempt to justify the recent, but controversial, innovation of the festivals of Yom Ha'atsmaut and Yom Yerushalayim.

Ezra/Nehemiah

This book contains numerous details concerning the laws enacted by Ezra and Nehemiah to combat the dire circumstances which they encountered when they returned to the Promised Land to build the Second Temple. Even though these laws are no longer pertinent, they are valuable in adding to our understanding of the authority of the Rabbis to impose laws upon the general populace.

WISDOM

WISDOM LITERATURE TEXTS INSTRUCT BY WAY OF A MORAL TALE OR A SERIES OF PARABLES OR FABLES. WISDOM LITERATURE IS OFTEN SAID TO CONTAIN A UNIVERSAL MESSAGE, SINCE IT IS SOMETIMES POSSIBLE FOR IT TO BE STUDIED INDEPENDENTLY OF THE RELIGION FROM WHICH IT COMES. WISDOM LITERATURE WILL PROVIDE ADVICE ON HOW TO CONDUCT ONESELF ETHICALLY AND MORALLY AND ON HOW TO FORM MEANINGFUL RELATIONSHIPS WITH OTHERS, PARTICULARLY WITHIN ONE'S OWN FAMILY AND IMMEDIATE SOCIAL CIRCLE.

Archeological findings led to the conclusion that wisdom literature as a particular literary style was common to many ancient religions. Early exponents of Form Criticism, however, did not identify wisdom literature as a separate literary style in the Tenach but included wisdom texts within the category of poetry.

In the twentieth century, however, archeologists discovered ancient Egyptian and Babylonian texts with similar themes to those found in *Job, Proverbs* and *Ecclesiastes*. This finding suggested that wisdom literature was common in the ancient world and led later scholars to classify Biblical wisdom literature separately.

Whereas the legal narratives in the Bible give specific commands from a position of authority, wisdom literature gives advice about:
- *refining one's character;*
- *controlling one's emotions;*
- *expressing one's true feelings appropriately;*
- *coping with the vicissitudes of daily life.*

Legal narratives define the behavioural boundaries within which Jewish life is lived; wisdom literature advises on the complexities of daily existence within those boundaries.

Location

In the Tenach, wisdom literature is primarily found in the Writings. The books of *Proverbs, Job* and *Ecclesiastes* (see Content of Tenach in Judaism AS for more details of contents) are considered the principal wisdom literature works. Unlike other books of the Bible, the wisdom texts make little mention of Israel's unique theological principles or historical experiences. Neither religious nor national identity is particularly stressed in these books. Instead, their emphasis is in the *ethical refinement of the individual.*

Proverbs

Proverbs examines the challenges one meets in the prime of life and guides one through the struggles to *develop moral discipline*, consistency in thought and action, *integrity* in personal relationships and, perhaps most important of all, *not losing sight of the real goals*. Although it contains occasional passages that refer to abstract ideals (perhaps the most frequent being the personification of wisdom as a woman), for the most part it is a practical book about everyday life and how to live it successfully. It extols wisdom and the benefits of being aware of it. It warns against being seduced by foolishness.

> *Go away from the presence of a foolish man... The wisdom of a shrewd man is*
> *to understand his way but the skepticism of fools is deceit.*[42]

Someone who is smart will accept the advice of the ones who know it already!

---

42   Proverrbs 14:7-8

Job

Job, by contrast, focuses on when *tragedy* strikes, highlighting the conflicting emotions and *challenges to one's faith* that may result. It expresses Man's inability to understand, which could lead to despair.

> Wisdom: from where does it come and how is it to be found? It is hidden from the eyes of all... Only G-d knows its paths.[43]

It does not explain the purpose of tragedy but shows how the individual may cope with tragedy and continue to live a positive life.

Ecclesiastes [Kohelet]

Ecclesiastes surveys the 'bigger picture' that only one who has already lived a life can appreciate. According to the Talmud, the point of Ecclesiastes is to teach that all is futile under the sun. One should therefore *ignore the physical pleasures and material accomplishments* of this world in order to put all one's efforts into that which is above the sun. This is summarized in the penultimate verse of the book:

> The end of the matter [when] all has been heard is to fear the Lord and observe His commandments; that is the whole duty of every person.

Those scholars who consider the **Creation** and **Garden of Eden** narratives to be mythological accounts would also view them as a form of wisdom literature. They would understand them as advisory texts relating to the universal issues of the nature of Man and his ultimate purpose in the universe. Similarly, the **Song of Songs**, besides being a great poetic work, could also be viewed as marriage guidance wisdom.

Wisdom literature continued to be produced in the post-Biblical era. There are also two major wisdom texts in the **Apocrypha**:

Ben Sira

This is a wisdom anthology, similar in style to Proverbs. It contains practical advice on inter-personal (particularly family) relationships, ethical business conduct and a variety of moral teachings. The book identifies G-d's wisdom with the Torah and fiercely opposes the rising tide of Hellenism, which led scholars to conclude it was written in the decades immediately before the Macabeean revolt, probably around 200-175 BCE.

The Wisdom of Solomon.

This work concentrates almost exclusively on the **foolishness of idolatry**. Although it has been ascribed to King Solomon by Christian scholars, it is not mentioned in the Talmud. Modern scholars believe it more likely to have been written in Alexandria in the Roman period, possibly by an early Christian scholar.

The **Talmud** also contains many wisdom narratives, the most influential being the Mishnah tractate **Ethics of the Fathers**. This contains advice on every conceivable area of private and communal life, gleaned from the sayings of the Rabbis of the Mishnaic period. Besides being essential elementary study for every Orthodox Jew, it is also recited at the end of the Sabbath afternoon service during the summer months.

---

43   Job 28: 20-23

LITURGY

LITURGY IS WHAT WE CALL THE LANGUAGE USED IN WORSHIP, IN WHICH WORDS ARE REPEATED ACCORDING TO A SET FORMULA. THIS GIVES THE WORSHIPPER THREE THINGS:

- a sense of communal identity with others saying the same words;

- a protective formal structure for worship;

- and a sense of occasion.

The Orthodox daily prayer service originates from the sixth century BCE, during the Babylonian exile. It is impossible to know with any certainty whether any of the Biblical texts were originally composed for the purpose of being words of prayer. A large part of the Jewish worship ritual, however, is based on Biblical sources. It is structured around the sacrificial ritual as described in the Torah.

The preliminary morning service outlines the daily sacrificial order with detailed references both to the Biblical sources (primarily in Leviticus and Numbers) and the Talmudic explanations of these rites. The purpose of this recital is to serve as a substitute for the sacrifices themselves. Each section concludes with a petition that *the offerings of our lips*[44] be accepted as a substitute for the actual offerings that can no longer be brought. It then concludes with a further petition for a speedy deliverance from exile and rebuilding of the Temple, that the sacrificial order may be restored as of old.

All the daily and festival prayers then continue with *chapters of song*, a series of liturgical recitals which make liberal use of the book of *Psalms* and regular references to verses from the *Prophets* that relate to the situation of living in exile. The high points of this section include the *Ashrei*,[45] an alphabet acrostic that extols G-d as provider of all and the *Song of the Red Sea*,[46] with which the section concludes.

The *three paragraphs of the Shema*[47] form the centerpiece of both the morning and evening services and, in both services, their concluding blessings lead directly into the Amidah, the silent prayer of eighteen blessings in which Jews beseech G-d for all their needs. *The Shema is the oldest fixed prayer.* Talmudic tradition states that it was recited twice daily from earliest Biblical times.

On *Shabbat, festivals* and *Rosh Chodesh*, there is an *additional service,* corresponding to the additional sacrifice offered in the Temple on those days. The main theme of this service is the desire for the rebuilding of the Temple and restoration of the sacrificial ritual.

The Amidah, together with Ashrei (but not the Shema) is also recited in the *afternoon service.* In the *evening service*, however, the Shema and the Amidah are recited, but not Ashrei. Every service ends with the *Aleinu* prayer which, according to Gaonic tradition, was composed by Joshua as he triumphantly led the Israelites across the River Jordan into the Promised Land. It comprises two paragraphs, the first emphasises the superiority of monotheism over all other forms of worship, the second of which contains a prayer that all humanity will one day acknowledge the sovereignty of G-d.

---

44   Hosea 14:3
45   Psalm 145
46   Exodus 15
47   Deuteronomy 6:4-9; 11:13-21; Numbers 15:37-41

In the Temple service, the daily sacrifice was accompanied by a *Psalm of Praise recited by* the Levites. It is now the accepted custom to recite this daily Psalm near the conclusion of the daily service. Each day has a different psalm. There are also special psalms to be recited on different festivals, on Rosh Chodesh and during the period of repentance that surrounds Rosh Hashanah and Yom Kippur.

From earliest times, it was decreed that *a portion of the Torah be associated with each week.* On Shabbat afternoon and on Monday and Thursday mornings, the first part of this portion is recited in the synagogue. On Shabbat morning, the whole portion is recited. The entire Torah is completed every year on Simchat Torah amidst great celebration.

Every Shabbat and festival morning, *a section from the Prophets* (called the *Haftorah*) which relates either to the weekly portion or to the respective festival is also recited. The Talmud states that this custom began during the Roman persecutions when it was forbidden to recite the Torah. An appropriate prophetic passage was selected as a substitute. The custom continued alongside the Torah recital after the persecutions ended.

In the Gaonic period (approx. 500-1000) there was a tradition for the *Rabbi to speak at the end of the service,* basing his talk on a text from *Writings* that in some way related to that week's Torah portion. In this way the unity and importance of all three sections of the Bible were highlighted. Many scholars believe that the modern practice for a Rabbi to deliver a sermon after the Shabbat or festival service is based upon this tradition.

The book of Jonah is recited as the Haftorah on the afternoon of *Yom Kippur.* One of the major themes of the book of Jonah is repentance. Many laws of repentance are derived from Jonah's prayer is the belly of the fish.[48] It is also the ultimate consolation of the sinner that sincere repentance is always accepted, no matter how wicked a person may have been. This is exemplified by the forgiveness of the idolatrous Ninevites.[49] That is why Jonah is recited on Yom Kippur.

The *five megillot* are also recited in full on special days in the calendar:

> On *Pesach,* which is compared to the betrothal of G-d and the Jewish People, ***Song of Songs***, which describes the love of a man [G-d] for his betrothed [Israel], is recited.

---

48   See Chapter 2
49   See Chapter 3

On *Shavuot,* which commemorates Israel's committing themselves to keep the Torah, *the book of Ruth,* which describes one woman's commitment to convert to Judaism, is recited.

On *Sukkot,* which abounds with food, drink, song and dance, *Ecclesiastes,* which reminds of the superiority of spiritual over physical pleasures, is recited.

On *Purim,* which commemorates Israel's deliverance from Persian anti-semetism, *the book of Esther,* which tells the Purim story, is recited.

On *Tisha b'Av,* which mourns the destruction of the Temple, *Lamentations,* a poetic description of the Babylonian conquest, is recited.

The book of Psalms in particular plays a very significant role in Jewish liturgy. Besides those Psalms recited daily as part of the formal services, many Orthodox Jews make a point of *reciting the whole book regularly.* In many communities, *Orthodox women* meet together regularly to recite sections of Psalms.

Every festival, a series of joyous Psalms called collectively *Hallel* is recited in the morning service. The Hallel recital is also included in the Pesach Haggadah. In some communities these Psalms are sung joyously, not just recited. A Psalm is also recited before the *Grace After Meals.*

Certain Psalms are recited upon *visiting a graveyard,* others as a petition for the *healing of the sick,* others as *expressions of thanks* in times of celebration.

Conclusion

The Tenach plays a major role in Jewish liturgy, but not the only role. Many important parts of Jewish liturgy, however, do not come from the Tenach.

The *Amidah* was composed by early Rabbinic scholars, as were the daily blessings and the Grace After Meals recited by observant Jews.

The beautiful poems that form the centerpiece of the Rosh Hashanah and Yom Kippur services, the mournful stanzas [called kinnot] chanted on Tisha b'Av and the various penitential [called selichot] prayers recited on fast days were all composed by medieval scholars.

Most of the Pesach Haggadah, the song/poems [called zemirot] of Shabbat, festivals and Chanukah, the wedding and funeral services are all vital parts of Jewish liturgy that have post-Biblical origins.

Despite this, however, it would be fair to conclude that the Tenach is the single most significant component of Jewish liturgy.

THEMES FROM
JEWISH SCRIPTURES:

COVENANT

EXPLAINING HOW THE CONCEPT OF COVENANT DEVELOPS THROUGH THE BIBLICAL PERIOD. UNDERSTANDING 8 DIFFERENT COVENANT TEXTS

- **ADAM**   - *Genesis 1:26-30*
- **NOAH**   - *Genesis 8:20-9:29*
- **ABRAHAM**   - *Genesis 12, 15. 17*
- **MOSES**   - *Exodus 19-24*
- **DAVID**   - *2 Samuel 7*
- **JEREMIAH**   - *Jeremiah 31*

WHAT IS A COVENANT?

In the Tenach, a covenant is an agreement between two sides. Unlike a partnership, however, where both sides have an equal commitment, a covenant involves different obligations for the two sides. *All the covenants we will study are between G-d and Man.* G-d's side of the covenant will typically be to provide all that the 'other half' of the covenant needs to fulfil their side. Also, unlike a partnership, if one side breaks the covenant the other side still remains bound by it. If, for example, Israel fails to keep her side, that does not mean that G-d is exempt from keeping His side. It just means that the way G-d keeps His side will change.

The Tenach often uses the expression 'to cut a covenant'. Possibly, this is because the ceremony accompanying the first covenant G-d made with Abraham was consecrated by Abraham cutting the carcasses of the animals and walking between them.

SUZERAINTY COVENANTS

Studies in the history of the Biblical period have established that the suzerainty covenant concept was common among the idolatrous nations amongst whom the Israelites lived. A suzerainty covenant is one in which *a more powerful country makes a pact with a weaker one* (often following victory in a war or to defend them against imminent invasion) agreeing to offer *protection in return for loyalty*, worship of their deity and/ or a payment of tribute. This is the type of covenant the Israelites were commanded not to offer to the Cana'anites when they entered the Land[50] and the one begrudgingly awarded the Gibeonites by Joshua[51].

Covenants made with G-d, however, while superficially similar to this, are not the same. Certainly, G-d provides the needs, including protection, of the other party and demands loyalty, through the observance of His commandments in return. When a weaker nation failed in its obligation to its protector, however, this usually led to its destruction or abandonment in return. G-d may punish those who violate His covenant, but He never abandons or destroys them.

---

50   *Deuteronomy 7:1-2*
51   *Joshua 9*

COVENANT SIGNS

A covenant may sometimes be accompanied by an external sign or token to *remind each party of its responsibilities*. The rainbow, for example, is a reminder of G-d's covenant with humanity in the days of Noah; circumcision is the sign of G-d's covenant with Abraham; and the Shabbat, according to Talmudic interpretation, is the sign of the Mount Sinai covenant. In each case, *the sign reassures*: G-d reassures Noah that He will never destroy the world again; He reassures Abraham that his descendants will have a unique role to play in the world; Israel, through its acceptance of the Torah, are reassured that this will be the vehicle through which the world's ultimate purpose will be fulfilled. At the same time, *the sign also symbolises responsibilities*: the seven colours of the rainbow remind the Noahides of their seven laws; circumcision highlights morality as the foundation of the Chosen People concept; Shabbat identifies the Jew as one whose entire life is governed by the laws of the Torah.

PROMISSORY COVENANTS

Biblical covenants will sometimes be 'cut' in the form of *a promise for something that will only happen in the future*. One feature of Abraham's covenant was the promise that, at some unspecified future date, G-d would establish His covenant with Abraham's descendants. This was only fulfilled 400 years later when G-d spoke to the Israelites at Mount Sinai. Another feature of this covenant is the assurance that the land of Cana'an would become the possession of his descendants. This was not fulfilled until 40 years after the revelation at Sinai when Joshua led the people into the land. Similarly, when making a covenant with King David, G-d promises that his son Solomon would build the Temple. He also assures him that legitimate kingship will always descend only from him.

In both cases, however, the promissory element, although very important, was *not the major theme of the covenant*. Abraham's covenant introduced the Chosen People concept to Judaism; David's covenant established the concept of kingship which would ultimately evolve into the Messianic concept. *Jeremiah* receives a prophecy covenant and this alone is *exclusively a promissory covenant*. It contains the promise to Jeremiah that, at the end of days, G-d will enter into a 'new' covenant with Israel.

The promissory elements of the respective covenants are unconditional. G-d promises Abraham that He will enter into a covenant with his descendants and the land would become their eternal possession. King David is assured that only his descendants would be Israel's rightful king. There will be an 'end of days' when G-d's promise to Jeremiah is realised.

This does not mean that promissory covenants are one-sided. *The conditional side of a promissory covenant, however, lies in the past not the future.* Abraham's and King David's previous worthiness had merited a covenant. Israel's 'chosenness' ensures a new covenant will be 'cut' at the end of days

CONCLUSION

Covenants are a very importance feature of the Tenach.

On the one hand, they provide the assurance of G-d's protection for those who are part of the covenant, even those who do not fulfil their covenantal responsibilities as they should. Being part of a covenant connects one to Israel's past and future, giving purpose and meaning to one's present.

At the same time, however, the covenant concept does impart responsibilities on each individual member of the covenant group. Violating the covenant may not lead to abandonment or destruction, but there are consequences to such unacceptable conduct.

The covenant concept, consequently, promotes the ideas of collective involvement and personal responsibility together with the security of divine care and supervision.

COVENANT WITH ADAM
Genesis 1:26-30

26 *And G-d said: let us make Adam in our image, as our likeness and they shall rule over the fish of the sea, the birds of the sky and over the animal(s) and all the earth and over every creeping thing that creeps on the earth.* **27** *And G-d created Adam in his image, in the image of G-d He created him, male and female He created them.* **28** *And G-d blessed them and said to them: be fruitful and multiply, fill the earth and subdue it and rule over the fish of the sea, the birds of the sky and over every living thing that moves on the earth.* **29** *And G-d said: behold, I have given you all vegetation yielding seed upon the surface of the entire earth and every tree that has seed yielding fruit; to you it shall be for food.* **30** *And to every beast on the land, to every bird of the sky and to everything that creeps on the earth, within which is a living soul, all greenery which is vegetation [is given] for food.*

RESPONSIBILITY NOT POWER

There is no reference to a covenant between G-d and Adam in the Torah. The first verse of this paragraph teaches, however, that, when G-d created Adam he had a purpose in mind. *G-d wanted Adam to rule over the world.* Since Adam is the first human, he represents the entire human race. This is a covenant with all human beings, represented by Adam. Those who understand the creation narrative as a myth would explain it as a tale through which the purpose of life is communicated.

The Talmud explains that, in Jewish law, *'ownership' is a responsibility not a power.* For example, the owner of a slave must provide him with food, shelter and protection and is forbidden to beat or otherwise mistreat him. It is forbidden to destroy even one's own possessions if they are still functional.[52] Similarly, Adam's ownership of the world is to be understood as a responsibility of *stewardship.* All G-d's creations have a useful function to perform. It is Adam's responsibility, therefore, to care for every part of creation and provide the means for each to fulfil its purpose in the world.

This teaches that *all human beings share a responsibility for the physical environment.* Ecological considerations demand that safeguards are taken to ensure that the beautiful world G-d created be maintained in all its splendour. This could be interpreted to mean that all nations have a responsibility to preserve the world's resources and to safeguard against pollution and the despoiling of places of natural beauty. Individuals can play their part by recycling waste, maintaining their own possessions and avoiding excess. Vandalism and littering would be particularly obvious violations of this responsibility.

The well-being of the animal world is also part of man's responsibility. Animals may be used for human needs, but *precautions must be put in place to guard against abuse.* Animals may be used for work, food and medical research. Those that spread disease, harm crops or other animals may be humanely put down. Factory farming excesses and arbitrary animal experimentation should be avoided, however. Hunting for sport and bullfighting are also considered violations of man's responsibility to maintain the animal world.

HUMILITY AND CONSIDERATION FOR OTHERS

The Talmud explains that it is impossible to comprehend the essence of G-d's being. All we can do is identify His attributes when He chooses to show them to us. *G-d will reveal to us those of His attributes that He wants us to emulate.* The first of these is found at the beginning of this paragraph.

---

52   *Based on TB Kiddushin 2a et al This is the law of ba'al tashchit – wilful destruction.*

Rashi is puzzled by the statement: let us make man [v.26]. Who is G-d talking to? He concludes that G-d is talking to the angels. Why did G-d need to consult the angels? Rashi explains that, of course G-d does not need their help. The angels are affected by the creation of Adam and so He confided in them before going ahead. *This shows G-d's attribute of humility* for, even though He did not need the angels help, G-d made them feel needed. *It teaches us to act humbly* and show consideration for the feelings of others.

EVERY PERSON IS UNIQUE

Adam was created in his image [v.27]. Who does the word his refer to? It cannot refer to G-d because it says immediately after this that Adam was created in the image of G-d. The Talmud states that it refers to Adam himself and teaches that **every human being is created in his/her own unique image.**[53] G-d has a special task for each person to perform in their lifetime, a task that nobody else can accomplish.

Modern scholars have understood this passage to be the source of *self-esteem*. If each human being is unique, each human being has their own unique role, unique contribution to make to the world that no other human being can make. This means that every single one of us is special, every single one of us is important, needed. Scientific advancement in the discovery of fingerprinting and DNA profiles has confirmed the physical uniqueness of each human being.

FREE WILL

Adam was also created in the image of G-d. In what way is a human being like G-d? It cannot refer to a physical likeness because G-d has no physical form, so it must refer to the soul. In what way is the human soul like G-d? In what way are human beings set aside and unlike any other of G-d's creations?

The Talmud[54] explains that, just as G-d has the ability to choose, so does a human being. All other creatures respond to their *instinct* and follow their desires. Human beings alone have the *free will* to overcome their desires and act from higher motives. With free will comes the ability to make decisions and the responsibility to stand by those decisions and accept the consequences of one's choices.

Rabbeinu Bachya in Duties of the Heart points out that *free will is the most important component of the human personality.* Only a free-willed creature is entitled to be rewarded for doing right or punished for doing wrong. An animal is purely physical and instinctively follows its body's desires; an angel is purely spiritual and instinctively obeys G-d's commands.

---

53   *This is based on an Aggadic Talmudic statement that G-d prepares a mould for each human being [see TB Ketubot 8a]*
54   *TB Bava Bathra 58a*

Human beings alone are uniquely composed of both the physical and the spiritual and have the ability to choose whether to live like an animal or like an angel. When human being succumb to their desires they resemble animals, but *they are worse than animals* for an animal cannot choose to be anything else. When human beings overcome their desires to follow G-d's will they act like angels, only they are greater than angels for they chose their actions. For this reason, Rabbeinu Bachya concludes, the human being is considered the crown of creation.

MALE AND FEMALE

The Hebrew word for a man is ish and for a woman is ishah. The word Adam means human being. The Torah states that Adam was created male and female. This indicates that the original human being created in the image of G-d was a combination of both male and female that only later was split into man and woman. No man or woman, consequently, can be a 'complete' human being without their 'other half'. It is G-d's plan, therefore, for *each man and woman to seek out and find their appropriate partner and make that*

'complete' relationship the basis of their whole lives.[55]

FINISH THE JOB

At the end of each component of creation, the Torah says: and G-d saw that it was good. This teaches that *only something that has been completed can be called 'good'.* The life of a human being should be filled by tasks to be accomplished. Once started, a task should be seen through to its end. Modern psychology has identified the failure to complete tasks as a sure sign of the lack of self-confidence. It causes people to lose belief in themselves, to view themselves as failures.[56]

55   *Midrash Genesis Rabba 8:1*
56   *Midrash Genesis Rabba 4:6*

CONCLUSION

There was no formal 'covenant' made with Adam. G-d created the world for a purpose, however, and it was to be the role of each human being **to** assume responsibility for G-d's creation. G-d's commands to Adam and His revealing of His attributes indicated what was expected of humanity. G-d also gave assurances that all their needs would be provided by Him. Although this is not a formal covenant, nevertheless the relationship between G-d and Adam fulfils all the criteria of a covenant relationship.

The Midrash compares the world to an orchestra. An orchestra contains many different instruments, each of which plays a unique and beautiful form of music. If all the instruments are just played haphazardly, however, and there is no harmony, all that will result is a deafening cacophony of sound. But once the conductor assumes his position and directs each instrument to begin and pause at the appropriate points then this horrible noise will be transformed into a beautiful symphony.

The world is exactly the same. Every creature has its own unique and wonderful contribution to make, but if left to their own devices they will just devour each other and destroy the world. The human being is like the conductor who supervises and directs all to co-operate and harmonise with each other to bring the world to completion.

COVENANT WITH NOAH
Genesis 8:20-9:29

8:20 *And Noah built an altar to G-d and took of every pure animal and of every pure bird and offered up completely burnt offerings upon the altar. 21 And G-d smelled the pleasant aroma and G-d said in His heart: I will not continue to curse the ground on account of man for the inclination of the heart of a person is evil from his youth; nor will I continue any more to smite all living beings as I have done. 22 Continuously, all the days of the earth: seedtime and harvest and cold and heat, summer and winter and day and night, they shall not cease.*

9:1 *And G-d blessed Noah and his sons and He said to them: be fruitful and multiply and fill the earth. 2 And the fear of you and the dread of you will be upon all the beasts of the earth and every bird of the heavens, in everything that creeps on the earth and in all the fish of the sea; into your hand they are given. 3 Every moving being that lives to you it shall be for food just like the vegetation; I have given to you everything. 4 Only the flesh with its soul, its blood [still in it] you shall not eat. 5 But your blood for your soul I will demand, from the hand of every living creature I will demand it; from the hand of a person, a man [who kills] his brother I will demand the soul of that person. 6 One who spills the blood of a person, through human [agency] his blood shall be shed for in the image of G-d He made [each] human being. 7 But [all of] you: be fruitful and multiply swarm over the land and multiply upon it. 8 And G-d said to Noah and to his sons saying: 9 And I, behold, I establish My covenant with you and your seed after you. 10 And with every living being that is with you: with the birds, animals and every beast of the land with you; of all that is going out of the ark, of every beast of the land. 11 And I will cause my covenant to be established with you: never again shall all flesh be cut off by the waters of the flood; there will not be another flood to destroy the land. 12 And G-d said: this is the sign of the covenant which I give between Me and you and every living being which is with you for all generations. 13 My bow I have put in the cloud and it shall be for a sign of the covenant between Me and the earth. 14 And it shall be when I bring clouds upon the earth that the bow will be seen in the clouds. 15 Then I will remember My covenant between Me and you and every living being among all flesh and the water will never again become a flood to destroy all flesh. 16 And the bow shall be in the clouds; I will see it [and] remember the eternal covenant between G-d and every living being among all flesh that is on the earth. 17 And G-d said to Noah: this is the sign of the covenant which I have established between Me and all flesh which is on the earth.*

18 *The sons of Noah who came out of the ark were Shem, Cham and Yafeth; Cham is the father of Canaan. 19 These three are the sons of Noah and from these the whole world spread out. 20 And Noah the man of the earth debased himself; he planted a vineyard. 21 And he drank from the wine and became drunk and uncovered himself inside his tent. 22 And Cham, who is the father of Canaan, saw his father's nakedness and told his two brothers outside. 23 Then Shem and Yafeth took a garment and placed it upon both their shoulders and walked backwards; they covered their father's nakedness [whilst] their faces were turned backwards; they did not see their father's nakedness. 24 Then Noah awoke from his wine and he knew what his youngest son had done to him. 25 And he said: cursed be Canaan: a servant of servants shall he be to his brothers. 26 And he said: blessed is G-d, the G-d of Shem; and Canaan shall be a servant to them. 27 May G-d expand Yafeth and may he dwell in the tents of Shem; and Canaan shall be a servant to them. 28 And Noah lived 350 years after the flood. 29 And all the days of Noah were 950 years and he died.*

WHY DID G-D DESTROY THE WORLD?

The Mishnah states:

> There were ten generations from Adam until Noah to highlight how patient He was for
> each generation rebelled against him until He brought a flood (to destroy them).[57]

Rashi asks why, after all that patience, did G-d finally decide to destroy the world in that generation? The answer, he says, is hinted at in the words of the Torah. It says: … the earth had become corrupt… and filled with robbery.[58]

When the people rebelled against G-d, worshipping idols, challenging His authority, G-d was patient. Once they were cruel to each other, however, that was different. *Patience is not a virtue when others are suffering*. Immediately, He decided to send the flood.

The flood narrative, which serves as an introduction to the covenant with Noah, teaches an important moral lesson. *Man's inhumanity to man represents the most serious desecration of his own purpose*. The flood is not to be understood as the jealous response of a vengeful G-d whose words have been ignored once too often. Instead, *the flood is a supreme act of justice*. It demonstrates that cruelty and selfishness have no part in G-d's world. The covenant with Noah would emphasise this principle.

NOAH OFFERS SACRIFICES

Immediately upon leaving the ark, Noah built an altar and offered sacrifices to G-d. It says that: G-d smelled the pleasant aroma and decided to make a covenant with Noah. *Why did Noah offer sacrifices?* What was it that G-d smelled? Why did this act trigger off the covenant?

In the ancient world, a sacrifice was a symbol of a person's commitment to G-d. The pagan nations used sacrifices to appease their idols. In Judaism, however, their purpose was completely different. The Hebrew word for sacrifice is korban which means literally come near. *A sacrifice is a method of expressing closeness to G-d* and is an expression of one's appreciation of G-d's goodness. Noah offered sacrifices as an expression of thanks for deliverance from the flood and a demonstration of commitment to G-d for the future.

From this, we can deduce that the pleasant aroma refers to Noah's intentions. G-d smelled, i.e. perceived, the aroma of Noah's good intentions. In this act, consequently, *Noah had earned the right to a covenant.*

---

57   *Pirkei Avos 5:2*
58   *Genesis 6:11*

ADAM'S COVENANT RENEWED

In some ways, the covenant with Noah is a renewal of the covenant with Adam. It also included the commandment to be fruitful and multiply and fill the earth. This indicates that the *purpose of the covenant would be the same as it was for Adam:* that the human race accepts responsibility for the world. *The means by which this would be accomplished, however, would be different.*

ANIMALS TO FEAR HUMANS

G-d now put into each animal an instinctive fear of humans. This further expands their rule over the animal world. Sforno points out that animals live by instinct, doing neither right nor wrong. The soul of an animal, consequently, always remains as pure as the day it was born. This gives animals an instinctive spiritual connection. Humans, by contrast, live by free-will. *An animal will therefore only fear a person who uses their free-will to do right* and be elevated above the animals. [Incidentally, this helps to understand the story of Daniel in the lion's den.]

MEAT PERMITTED FOR FOOD

The Talmud gives two reasons for why meat became permitted for food after the flood:

1) *Reduced lifespan:* Before the flood, people lived many centuries. After the flood, life expectancy would be reduced to less than a hundred years. Less time was now available and so *greater energy would be needed* to achieve life's tasks. A more vivifying diet would therefore be necessary.

2) *Greater entitlement:* The world was only saved from complete destruction by the merit of Noah and his family, so they were more entitled to be on the earth than animals, which were only saved for their sakes. This means that there is a greater entitlement to use animals for human needs than there was before the flood.

THE SEVEN NOAHIDE LAWS

From the text of Genesis 9:4-7, the Talmud derives the laws which would define G-d's expectations of humanity for all future generations. These seven laws illuminate the human responsibility for the world:

1. Do not murder

Respect the integrity of each individual. This *establishes the basic human rights of all* to existence, regardless of race, colour or creed.

2. Do not commit adultery

Respect the integrity of the family unit. This establishes *a code of morality* and the necessity of marriage. There cannot be adultery if there are no marriage laws.

3. Do not steal
Respect the integrity of others' possessions. This establishes the need for *honesty in human relationships*. It also hints at the importance of *personal responsibility* for providing one's material needs. There can be no theft if there is no ownership.

4. Do not worship idols
Respect the integrity of G-d. This establishes the need for a knowledge and understanding of *G-d's complete mastery* of all the forces of the universe.

5. Do not blaspheme (take G-d's Name in vain)
Respect the integrity of the relation with G-d. This establishes a concept of respecting those greater than ourselves and promotes *humility.*

6. Do not eat the limb of a live animal
Respect the integrity of the animal world. This establishes the principle that it is forbidden to cause any *unnecessary suffering to animals*. It effectively prohibits any wanton acts of cruelty, e.g. fox-hunting, bullfighting, random vivisection.

7. Establish courts of law
Respect the integrity of the community. This establishes the responsibility of each community to appoint three legal bodies: a *government* to determine the law; a *police force* to enforce the law; *courts* to punish those who break the law. In this way, each community will be able to maintain a system of justice which protects all those who abide by its laws.

THE RAINBOW – THE SIGN OF THE COVENANT
The rainbow is to be a sign of allegiance to the covenant both for G-d and for humans.

It is a sign for G-d because the bow (symbolising a weapon of destruction) faces away from the world. This suggests that G-d's 'arrows' will be directed away from the world. When seeing a rainbow, one is reminded of G-d's promise not to destroy the world again. Who knows? Perhaps that is the only reason we are not being destroyed at this moment. The Talmud states, consequently, that *one who sees a rainbow should repent their sins*. Also, there is a blessing to be recited upon seeing a rainbow.

It is a sign for humans for a rainbow is a natural phenomenon whose main component is water. The same water that destroyed the world can also produce an object of outstanding beauty. Although water can destroy life it is also the source of life for nothing can exist without water.

Why was the rainbow chosen to be the sign?

The Talmud explains that the rainbow symbolises the fact that *nature is the servant of humanity; humanity is not the servant of nature*. If people fulfil their side of the covenant, G-d gives an assurance that all their needs will be provided by nature. Only when the covenant is violated is nature something to be feared. All natural disasters such as earthquakes, tornadoes and volcanic eruptions are to be understood as signs of the failure to maintain the covenant G-d made with Noah.

In describing the greatness of *Rabbi Shimon bar Yochai*, the Talmud states that the merit of his good deeds outweighed the sins of the entire generation to such a degree that no rainbow was seen in the sky throughout his life. That is why there is a custom for children to play with bows of *Lag b'Omer*, the anniversary of his death.

CONCLUSION

The covenant with Noah established the moral and legal structure upon which all human civilisations would be based. It was never revoked and remains, according to Judaism, binding upon all Gentiles. The Talmud states: the righteous of all nations inherit a portion in the world to come. Who are the righteous ones? Those Gentiles whose lives are based on the seven Noahide laws.

COVENANT WITH ABRAHAM - 1
Genesis 12

1 *And G-d said to Abram: go for yourself from your land, from your birthplace and from your father's house to the land which I will show you. 2 And [there] I will make you into a great nation; and I will bless you and make your name great and you will be a blessing. 3 And I will bless those who bless you and the one who curses you I will curse; and through you will all the families of the earth be blessed. 4 So Abram went as G-d had spoken to him and Lot went with him; and Abram was 75 years old went he left Haran. 5 and Abram took Sarai his wife and Lot his nephew and all their possessions which they had accumulated and the souls which they made in Haran; and they left to go to the land of Canaan and they came to the land of Canaan. 6 And Abram passed through the land as far as the place Shechem, until the plain of Moreh; the Canaanites were then still in the land. 7 And G-d appeared to Abram and He said: to your seed I will give this land; so he built an altar there to G-d who had appeared to him. 8 Then he relocated from there to the mountains to the east of Beit-Eil and pitched his tent [with] Beit-Eil to the west and Ai to the east; and he built there an altar to G-d and he called out in the name of G-d. 9 Then Abram travelled [on] going towards the south. 10 Then there was a famine in the land so Abram went down to Egypt to sojourn there for the famine was very severe in the land. 11 And it was, when he was close to entering Egypt that he said to Sarai his wife: behold, now I know that you are a woman of beautiful appearance. 12 And it shall be, when the Egyptians see you that they shall say: this is his wife; then they shall kill me but you they will let live. 13 Please say you are my sister that it may go well with me for your sake that I may live on account of you. 14 But it was, when Abram came to Egypt that the Egyptians saw [that] the woman was very beautiful. 15 The officers of Pharaoh saw her and praised her to Pharaoh and the woman was taken to Pharaoh's palace. 16 And he treated Abram well on account of her and he acquired flocks and herds, donkeys, servants and maidservants, female donkeys and camels. 17 Then G-d afflicted Pharaoh and his household with severe afflictions on account of Sarai wife of Abram. 18 So Pharaoh summoned Abram and said: what is this that you have done to me; why did you not tell me that she was your wife? 19 Why did you say: she is my sister; that I would take her to me as a wife; and now, here is your wife: take [her] and go. 20 And Pharaoh commanded men concerning him that they escort [out of the country] him and his wife and all that was his.*

WHY DID G-D CHOOSE ABRAHAM?

The Mishnah states:

> There were ten generations from Noah until Abraham to highlight how patient He was for each generation rebelled against him until Abraham came and received the reward of them all.[59]

So elevated was Abraham's commitment to G-d that *his merit outweighed the collective sins of the ten generations since the flood* and consequently atoned for them all.

The Midrash[60] describes how Abraham's uniqueness was not just that he believed in G-d, for there had been others who had believed in G-d before him. Abraham displayed three principal qualities:

ONE: Abraham was able to overcome an environment of idolatry and work out by himself that there was only one G-d.

TWO: Not only this, but he displayed the courage to defend monotheism against idolatry even putting his own life at risk.

THREE: Finally, he dedicated his life to influencing all around him to embracing monotheism.

This covenant was entered into in four stages. Abraham successively fulfils each of G-d's requirements as outlined in this chapter.

STAGE ONE – THE TASK: NO OTHER COMMITMENTS

G-d's first instruction was to leave land, birth-place and father's house. A question: logically, shouldn't these three 'departures' be written the other way round? It is not the physical departure that is being emphasised here, however, but the emotional departure.[61]

WHY LEAVE YOUR LAND?

A person is attached to the culture and emotional values of the country in which they grow up. But G-d's values must come before his country's values.

WHY LEAVE YOUR BIRTH-PLACE?

A person has an even stronger attachment to the city or community in which they grew up. Attachment to G-d must take precedence over these attachments

.WHY LEAVE YOUR FATHER'S HOUSE?

Even stronger than this is the natural bond of love with members of one's own family. Love of G-d must be greater even than love of one's family.

---

59   *Pirkei Avos 5:2*
60   *Genesis Rabba 38*
61   Ramban: Genesis 12:1

The lesson of this first stage has been relevant for Jews in many generations who, due to anti-semitism and persecution, were forced to leave countries they had lived in for generations or were suddenly rejected by their own villagers/townsfolk with whom they had always lived together peacefully. Sometimes, religious Jews were even ostracised by their own families for staying loyal to Torah law, despite the many hardships it entailed.

STAGE ONE – THE REWARD: THE PROMISED LAND

G-d promised Abraham his descendants would become a great nation and inherit the Land that I will show you. He had no idea where he was going when he left. He was also warned that the reward would not be seen in his lifetime. This highlights another aspect of the covenant concept. *Abraham's primary concern was with future generations, not with himself.* If he had laid the foundations for them to succeed, that was reward enough. This has been the principal value of Jewish family life throughout the generations.

G-d also promised that: I will bless those who bless you and the one who curses you I will curse. Many scholars noted how *countries treating Jews well tend to prosper and those who persecute the Jews soon lose their prosperity.* Even in modern times, the richest country in the world (the U.S.A.) is also the most tolerant of its Jewish population.

STAGE TWO – THE TASK: OUTREACH

When Abraham and Sarah left, it says they were accompanied by the souls they had made in Haran. The Midrash asks: How could they have made souls? It answers that this refers to those people who had been influenced to forsake their idolatrous practices and join them.[62] *It was this concern for others that is traditionally believed to have differentiated Abraham from Noah,* whose righteousness was limited to himself and his family.

STAGE TWO – THE REWARD: THE CHOSEN PEOPLE

It was this concern for others that was to be the most important aspect of the Chosen People concept. *Abraham and his descendants were to be the role models for all nations* for G-d's purpose in creation. Abraham was promised a special relationship that G-d would enter into with his future descendants. This special relationship would exist for all time, since it was based on the merit of Abraham, not on the merit of his descendants.

---

62   *Genesis Rabba 39:14; see also TB Sanhedrin 99b*

STAGE THREE – THE TASK: COMING CLOSE TO G-D

When Abraham reached Cana'an and passed through the land, G-d appeared to him again to confirm that it was this land that his descendants would inherit. Abraham then built an altar as an expression of his appreciation for all that G-d had done for him. Animal sacrifice was a common form of worship at this time. The idolatrous nations saw sacrifices as ends in themselves, the bringing of the sacrifice being itself an act of righteousness. Just like Noah, Abraham realised that *sacrifices were a means of coming close to G-d when brought with the correct intention*, in the same way that sincere prayer is nowadays. The word used for sacrifices in the Torah is korban which comes from the root karav which means to come close.

STAGE THREE – THE REWARD: G-D'S PERSONAL CARE

When Abraham's descendants received the Torah, it contained a system of worship which incorporated both sacrifices and prayers. *Those who availed themselves of this worship structure sincerely were assured of G-d's personal supervision* of their affairs. This concept (known as hashgachah pratis in Hebrew) is considered a fundamental component of Jewish belief.

STAGE FOUR – THE TASK: MAINTAINING THE FAITH

Shortly after this a famine hit the land. Most commentaries consider this a test for Abraham. G-d had made him leave everything behind to come to a strange land. Almost immediately, he had to leave to go down to Egypt to beg for food. It must have seemed illogical to him. *Why had G-d brought him here if it was impossible for him to live here?* Abraham was being taught that sometimes G-d does not reveal His purpose to us. That is when our absolute belief in Him and the innate goodness of all His actions is required.

Abraham and Sarah also had to cope with the realities of Egyptian life. *The Egyptians were an immoral people and Sarah was a very beautiful woman.* They would surely abduct and abuse her. The Midrash says that Abraham hid her in a trunk but the Egyptians found her and took her to Pharaoh. Why didn't they keep her as a slave for themselves?

The Midrash explains that, when they saw how beautiful she was they were afraid that, if Pharaoh found out about her, he would punish them for not bringing her to him![63] This incident gives us a picture of the kind of world Abraham lived in. He was surrounded by cruel and selfish people with no regard for others. Had they realised he was Sarah's husband, they would surely have murdered him. That is why he had to pretend she was his sister.

---

63   *Midrash Tanchuma 5*

STAGE FOUR – THE REWARD: ALL IS RESTORED

In Egyptian law, women were property like cattle or camels. Pharaoh consequently 'paid' Abraham for his 'sister'. Abraham dare not turn down Pharaoh's offer or he would be killed. In this way, G-d caused Abraham to become very rich through the famine. Sarah also was not harmed. Whenever Pharaoh tried to come near her, G-d sent a terrible plague upon him and his entire household.

In his anger and frustration, Pharaoh blames Abraham for not telling him she was his wife (conveniently forgetting what would have happened if he had!). As with all wicked men, Pharaoh sees blame everywhere except with himself. But Abraham's faith in G-d was vindicated. He returned to Cana'an a far wealthier and respected person than he had ever been before in his life.

CONCLUSION

The first part of the covenant with Abraham establishes the concept of the Chosen People and how they are required to live. They are promised a holy land as an eternal possession and they are to be an example to all of how to live with G-d and with each other both in the good times and in the bad times.

COVENANT WITH ABRAHAM - 2
Genesis 15

1 *After these things, the word of G-d came to Abram in a vision saying: do not fear Abram, I am a shield for you; your reward is very great. 2 And Abram said: my Lord G-d what can you give me for I go childless and the steward of my house is Eliezer of Damascus? 3 And Abram said: behold, to me you have not given seed so surely the [steward] of my house will inherit from me. 4 Suddenly the word of G-d [came] to him saying: this [one] shall not inherit from you but [the one] who comes out from your loins, he will inherit from you. 5 And He brought him outside and He said: gaze now to the heavens and count the stars if you are able to count them; and He said to him: so will be your seed. 6 And he trusted in G-d and He accounted it to him as [an act of] righteousness. 7 And He said to him: I am G-d who brought you out from Ur of the Chaldees to give this land to you to possess it. 8 And he said: my Lord G-d how can I [really] know that I will inherit it? 9 Then He said to him: bring [lit: take] to me three calves and three goats and three rams, a turtle-dove and a young dove. 10 And he brought [lit: took] all these to Him and he split them in the centre and placed each part opposite its kind but the bird[s] he did not split. 11 Then a vulture came down upon the carcasses but Abram drove them away. 12 And it was as the sun was setting that a deep sleep fell upon Abram and behold: a dread, a great darkness fell upon him. 13 And He said to Abram: know [with certainty] that your descendant[s] will be stranger[s] in a land which is not theirs; they will enslave them and afflict them [for] four hundred years. 14 But also the nation that shall enslave them I shall judge and afterwards they shall go out with great wealth. 15 And you shall come to your fathers in peace; you shall be buried at a good old age. 16 And the fourth generation shall return here for the iniquity of the Amorite shall not be complete until then. 17 And it was that the sun had set and there was [an intense] darkness: suddenly [there appeared] a furnace of smoke and a flame of fire which passed between these pieces. 18 On that day G-d made [lit: cut] a covenant with Abram saying: to your descendants I have given this land from the river of Egypt to the great river, the River Euphrates. 19 [Including the lands of] the Kenites, Kenizites and the Kadmonites. 20 And [the lands of] the Hittites, Perizites and the Rephaim. 21 And [the lands of] the Amorites, Canaanites, Girgashites and the Jebusites.*

WHY WAS ABRAHAM AFRAID?

This chapter opens with G-d telling Abraham: do not fear. What was Abraham afraid of?

ANSWER 1: HE WAS AFRAID FOR HIMSELF

In the previous chapter, Abraham had miraculously defeated the confederation of four kings who had taken Lot, his nephew, a prisoner. The Midrash[64] explains that G-d established this covenant in response to Abraham's fears. Some say he feared that *he had inadvertently killed righteous people* in this battle and he would be punished for this. Others say he feared that the miracles performed by G-d to help him win had *used up all the merit* he had accumulated in his life.

G-D RESPONDS: DO NOT BE AFRAID

G-d's answer is an indication that his fears are unfounded. On the one hand, *I am a shield to you* guaranteeing that no righteous people died by his hand. On the other hand, *your reward is very great* for no personal merit was 'used up' by the miracles performed for him. This was because Abraham went to war to save Lot, not for his own personal benefit.

ANSWER 2: HE WAS AFRAID FOR HIS DESCENDANTS

The Midrash continues: G-d had made a covenant with Abraham, assuring him that his descendants would be a great nation, but *he had no children!* Would the covenant be fulfilled through his closest blood relative, his nephew Lot, even though Lot was not worthy? Or would it be fulfilled through his servant Eliezer, who was worthy but not a relative?

G-D RESPONDS: PROMISE #1

G-d promised him that the covenant would be fulfilled through neither! *He would indeed have a son through whom the covenant would be fulfilled.* Not only that, but his descendants would be as numerous as the stars. Abraham did not ask for a sign that this promise would come true.

G-D RESPONDS: PROMISE #2

G-d then made a second promise to Abraham.. He promised him that *He would give this land to his descendants as a possession.* This implies that it would always belong to them. This time, Abraham did ask for a sign that this promise would come true.

PROBLEM: *Why did Abraham ask for a sign for the second promise, but not for the first promise? The fulfilment of the first promise would be far more miraculous!*

---

64   *Genesis Rabba 44:5 et al*

THE REAL REASON WHY ABRAHAM WAS AFRAID?

If G-d was promising an eternal covenant with his descendants, Abraham had no reason to doubt that it would really happen, so he had no need for a sign. Similarly, he did not doubt that G-d would give his descendants the land. But *suppose, at some time in the future, his descendants would sin* and no longer merit to remain in the land. What then?

G-D'S ASSURANCE:
THE COVENANT BETWEEN THE PARTS

G-d told Abraham to take three calves, three rams, three goats, a dove and a turtle-dove. These were the only animals and birds permitted for use as sacrifices that Abraham's descendants would bring to atone for their sins, thus avoiding exile from the land. The Midrash[65] explains the significance of these animals:

Three calves correspond to three calves bought as atonement offerings: on Yom Kippur; when a person is found murdered in a field[66]; where the Sanhedrin[67] mistakenly permits something which carries a penalty of the soul being cut off[68];

Three goats correspond to three different times when goats are used a sin offerings;

Three rams correspond to two different categories of guilt offerings[69] and the sin offering of the individual.

Abraham was then told to cut the animals in half and lay each piece opposite its corresponding part, but he was to leave the birds whole.

Abraham is given two assurances:

In the land: When his descendants take possession of the land, the sacrificial worship procedure will enable them to be inspired to atone for their sins and remain in the land.

In exile: Even when they are punished by exile and the sacrifices are taken away from them, G-d will still be with them. *When the animals are cut up, they represent the mighty empires that were able to defeat and exile Israel:* Assyria, Babylonia and Rome. They too will ultimately be destroyed but Israel, symbolised by the birds which were not cut up, will survive them all.

---

65   *Genesis Rabba 44:14*

66   *Deuteronomy 21. The murderer is unknown and the Rabbinical court of the town closest to where the body was found must bring a sacrifice of atonement.*

67   *The highest Rabbinical court.*

68   *Leviticus 4:13. For example, they ruled that something which, unknown to them, contained chametz was permitted to be eaten on Pesach.*

69   *Unlike sin offerings, which are brought for accidental transgressions, guilt offering are brought for deliberately transgressing certain commandments.*

Just as a bird is weak and defenceless in comparison to an animal, so will Israel be at the mercy of the nations throughout the exile, dependant upon G-d to ensure their survival.

Abraham then fell into a deep sleep, during which G-d gives him a prophetic vision of the future. *He was shown how his descendants would go down to Egypt and be redeemed after 400 years.*[70] He was shown the period of Israel's possession of the land, symbolised by the taking of the animals, and G-d's protection during the exile, symbolised by the cutting up of the animals.

When Abraham awoke, a fire came down from heaven and consumed the animals, just as the fire on the sacrificial altar will consume Israel's sacrifices to grant them atonement from their sins. *The fire also symbolised the destruction of the nations who persecute Israel during their exile.* Thus Abraham was assured of G-d's protection for his descendants throughout their history.

---

70   *Midrash Seder Olam uses the chronology of the Torah to calculate that the exodus from Egypt happened exactly 400 years after the birth of Isaac.*

COVENANT WITH ABRAHAM - 3
Genesis 17

1 *And it was [when] Abram was 99 years old that G-d appeared to Abram and He said to him: I am Eil Shaddai; walk before Me and be perfect. 2 And I will place my covenant between Me and you and I will increase you very, very much. 3 And Abram fell on his face and G-d spoke to him saying. 4 [As] for Me, here is My covenant with you and you shall be the father of a multitude of nations. 5 No longer will your name be called Abram but your name will be Abraham for I have made you the father of a multitude of nations. 6 And I will cause you to be exceptionally fruitful; I will make you [into] nations and kings will go forth from you. 7 and I will cause my covenant to be established between Me and you and your offspring after you throughout their generations as an eternal covenant, to be a G-d to you and to your offspring after you. 8 And I shall give to you and to your offspring after you the land of your sojourning: all the land of Canaan for an eternal possession and I shall be a G-d to them. 9 And G-d said to Abraham: and [as] for you, you shall keep my covenant, both you and your offspring after you throughout their generations. 10 This is My covenant that you shall keep between Me and you and your offspring after you: every male of you shall be circumcised. 11 And you shall circumcise the flesh of your foreskin and it shall be a sign of the covenant between Me and you. 12 At eight days old every male amongst you shall be circumcised throughout your generations [including both] those born in [your] house and those purchased for money from any stranger who is not your offspring. 13 [Both] those born in your house and those purchased for money must be circumcised; My covenant shall be in your flesh for an eternal covenant. 14 But an uncircumcised male, one of whom the flesh of his foreskin will not be circumcised: that soul shall be cut off from its people; he has invalidated My covenant. 15 And G-d said to Abraham: your wife Sarai, do not call her name Sarai but Sarah [shall be] her name. 16 And I shall bless her and I shall give to you a son from her; I will bless her that she shall be [the source of] nations; kings of countries shall [rise] from her. 17 Then Abraham fell on his face and he laughed; and he thought in his heart: from a 100 year old shall there be born; shall Sarah who is 90 give birth? 18 So Abraham said to G-d: would that Ishmael live before You. 19 But G-d said: indeed Sarah your wife will bear you a son and you will call his name Isaac [Heb: Yitzchok:- he will laugh] and I shall cause My covenant to be fulfilled with him, an eternal covenant for his offspring after him. 20 As for Ishmael, I have heard you: behold, I have blessed him and will make him fruitful and cause him to increase very, very much; he will bear twelve princes and I will make him into a great nation. 21 But my covenant I will establish with Isaac that Sarah will bear to you at this appointed time in the next year. 22 When He finished to speak with him, G-d ascended from upon Abraham. 23 Then Abraham took Ishmael his son and all [those] born in his household and all those purchased with his money, all the male [members] of Abraham's household and he circumcised the flesh of their foreskin on that very day just as G-d had spoken with him. 24 And Abraham was 99 years old when he circumcised the flesh of his foreskin. 25 And Ishmael his son was thirteen years old when he circumcised the flesh of his foreskin. 26 On that very day Abraham and Ishmael his son were circumcised. 27 And all the men of his household, [those] born in the household and [those] purchased with money from a stranger were circumcised with him.*

THE COMPLETION OF THE COVENANT

In this chapter we have the final component of G-d's covenant with Abraham. G-d commands him to walk before Me and be perfect. How is it possible to command a person to be perfect? Rashi explains this to mean being wholehearted in his commitment to following G-d's ways, i.e. with a perfect desire. We learned in the Covenant with Adam that the crucial difference between human beings and animals was free-will. Whereas animals will instinctively follow their desires at all times, human beings have the choice to resist their desires in order to do what is right. The final part of Abraham's covenant was an instruction to *commit himself to control his desires*. This idea was explained by Rabbi Aryeh Carmell, a twentieth century scholar, in the following way:

> *Being whole does not mean being perfect. Nobody is perfect. It means being single-minded – wholehearted. If one is tired of being pulled this way and that by his inner urges and ardently desires to have a single aim and to pursue it with all his heart–then he is a candidate for a covenant with G-d... [and] it was for this purpose that [they] were given [the land of] Israel – to show how every aspect of a society and a civilisation can be built up upon this wholesome base.*[71]

G-d made numerous promises to Abraham in return:

He will be the father of a multitude of nations:

This is symbolised by the changing of his name from Abram to Abraham which, in Hebrew, is an abbreviation of the phrase av hamon goyim, the Hebrew for father of a multitude of nations. This could be said to have been fulfilled through not just Jews but Christians and Moslems also identifying Abraham as the founding father of their religion.

An eternal covenant will be made with his descendants:

This was fulfilled when G-d made a covenant with the Israelites at Mount Sinai. He gave Israel the Torah through which they, the descendants of Abraham, would have an eternal bond with G-d throughout their generations.

The land would be an eternal possession of his descendants:

This is understood to mean that once the Israelites took possession of the land it would remain their 'right' to live there for all time. G-d could remove their right to sovereignty (as He did during the Babylonian and again during the Roman periods) but *it would always be a mitzvah for Jews to live in the land of Israel.* Also, the right to possess this land would never pass to any other nation.

---

71   *Masterplan (Feldheim Publishers, 1985) p,228*

CIRCUMCISION: THE SIGN OF THE COVENANT

G-d commanded Abraham to circumcise himself and all the male members of his household and every newborn male after eight days. Those that remain uncircumcised are not to be considered part of the people. This was to be the sign of G-d's covenant with Abraham's descendants for all time.

WHY IS CIRCUMCISION THE SIGN?

One of the reasons why circumcision is the sign of the covenant is that *it symbolises Israel's role*. Just as G-d created the world and left a small amount for humans to do to complete the creation,[72] so is a baby boy born almost complete with just a small fixture needing to be done to complete his entrance into the Jewish community.

WHY IS CIRCUMCISION ON THAT PART OF THE BODY?

G-d could have formed newborn boys to require a small part of any limb to be removed so the place chosen for circumcision must be significant. *The primary challenge of Abraham's covenant is to overcome one's desires.* The desire for immorality is considered the strongest of all the physical desires. At the same time, the correct channelling of this drive provides the basis for a happy marriage and is an essential for producing families.

The symbolism of circumcision is two-fold. Firstly, the removal of the foreskin warns that the covenant cannot be fulfilled unless desires are controlled. Secondly, it indicates that, *by exercising that control, one actually becomes the master of one's desires* and is able to use them to increase one's pleasure and fulfilment. This is beautifully described by Rabbi Aryeh Carmell:

> When the Torah was given [it] warned not to copy the immoral practices of the surrounding cultures. We now live in a time when very similar warnings need to be given. In the so-called civilised world in which we live, the number of divorces and broken homes is growing by leaps and bounds. One would think that civilisation would lead to happiness and satisfaction, but we see that this is not the case. Circumcision bids us to stand back and consider how ludicrous this is. It teaches us that permissiveness – that is, selfishness – actually restricts our lives and happiness[73]

WHY IS CIRCUMCISION THE OBLIGATION OF THE PARENT?

Children need guidance and direction to develop healthily toward maturity. Psychologists have demonstrated that, when children are given sensible 'boundaries' to their behaviour, they develop self-confidence from their knowledge of what they can/cannot do. In later life, they are more able to distinguish between right and wrong. This in turn creates the means for them to become caring adults, able to consider the needs of others but at the same time capable of becoming self-reliant.

---

72   *See Covenant with Adam for details*
73   *Masterplan p. 230*

It is therefore *the parents' responsibility to provide the certainties and securities of the young child's environment.* Circumcision symbolises the crucial role of parents in the raising of their children.

WHY NOT LET CHILDREN DECIDE FOR THEMSELVES?

Some might say that children should wait until they are old enough to decide for themselves whether or not they want to enter the covenant. Traditional Jews would not agree with this for the reasons outlined above and also because circumcision is not the covenant, it is the sign of the covenant. When children are old enough to question and think for themselves, they are encouraged to do so. *Ultimately, therefore, everybody is given the opportunity to decide for themselves* whether or not to live according to the covenant.

WHY IS CIRCUMCISION ON THE EIGHT DAY?

In Kabbalah [Jewish mysticism] the number 6 represents the physical world since there are six sides to a three-dimensional object. The number 7 represents a living, physical being since it has a functioning 'inside' [the soul]. The number 8, consequently, represents that which is 'beyond physical existence', i.e. spiritual existence. *Circumcision, consequently, is performed on the eighth day to symbolically indicate that the child's purpose in life is more than merely achieving physical, material goals.* One who enters Abraham's covenant gives precedence to the pursuit of spiritual goals.

CIRCUMCISION: THE CAPACITY FOR CHANGE

Just as the act of circumcision affects a physical change to the body, so does it symbolise the potential of a human being to change for the better. Circumcision is one of the clearest symbols of the principle that a human being must continually strive for self-improvement. The Talmud relates the following tale:

> The Romans strongly objected to circumcision. This is the body that the gods have given you, they reasoned. It is blasphemous to think that man can improve on that which the gods have produced.
>
> The evil Turnus Rufus once tried to trap Rabbi Akiba. He asked him: Which is better Rabbi, that which G-d makes or that which man makes? But Rabbi Akiba sensed the trap and replied immediately: Without a doubt, that which man makes!
>
> Turnus Rufus was shocked. How can you say that? Surely the works of G-d are greater than the works of man. Rabbi Akiba excused himself and returned shortly. In one hand, he held some ears of corn, in the other a cream cake. Well, Turnus Rufus, which would you prefer to eat - the works of G-d or the works of man?

This story illuminates the significance of circumcision. A human being is born as the 'raw material' that has to be worked upon and improved, first by one's parents and then by oneself, in order to become a fitting member of the covenant.

COVENANT WITH MOSES - 1
Exodus 19

1 *In the third month after the children of Israel went out from the land of Egypt, on that day, they came to the Sinai desert. 2 They travelled from Rephidim to the desert of Sinai and encamped; Israel encamped opposite the mountain. 3 Then Moses went up to G-d and G-d called to him from the mountain saying: so shall you say to the house of Jacob and tell to the children of Israel. 4 You have seen what I have done to Egypt and how I bore you upon eagle wings and brought you to Me. 5 And now, if you hearken to My voice and keep my covenant, you shall be my special possession among all the nations for all the earth is mine. 6 And you shall be to me a kingdom of priests and a holy nation; these are the words you must speak to the children of Israel. 7 So Moses came and summoned the elders of the people and set before them all these words that G-d had commanded him. 8 Then all the people answered together and said: All which G-d has spoken, we will do; then Moses brought back the words of the people to G-d. 9 And G-d said to Moses: Behold, I come to you in a dense cloud so that the people hear when I speak to you that they will also always believe in you; Moses then told G-d the words of the people. 10 And G-d said to Moses: Go down to the people and sanctify them today and tomorrow and they shall wash their garments. 11 And let them be ready on the third day; for on the third day G-d will come down before the eyes of all the people on Mount Sinai. 12 Set limits for the people all around the mountain and tell them: take care not to go up the mountain or even to touch its edge; whoever touches the mountain shall die. 13 No hand shall touch it; he shall be stoned or cast down, whether animal or man, he shall not live; when the ram's horn blows they may go up to the mountain. 14 Then Moses came down from the mountain to the people and he sanctified the people and they washed their garments. 15 And he said to the people: be ready by the [end of] three days; do not approach a woman. 16 And it was on the third day as morning broke that there was thunder and lightning and a heavy cloud over the mountain, and the sound of the shofar becoming stronger so that all the people in the camp trembled. 17 But Moses brought the people from the camp towards G-d and they stood at the foot of the mountain. 18 Mount Sinai was engulfed in smoke for G-d came down upon it in fire; its smoke rose like the smoke of a furnace and the whole mountain trembled greatly. 19 The shofar sound increased in strength; Moses spoke and G-d answered him in a voice. 20 Then G-d came down to the top of Mount Sinai; G-d summoned Moses to the top of the mountain, and Moses went up. 21 Then G-d said to Moses: go down and warn the people lest they break through toward G-d to see and many of them will fall. 22 And also the priests who come close to G-d must sanctify themselves lest G-d make a breach against them. 23 Moses said to G-d: The people cannot go up to Mount Sinai for You have warned us saying: set limits around the mountain to make it sacred. 24 And G-d said to him: go, descend and then you shall come up and Aaron with you, but the priests and the people must not break through to go up to G-d; else he will vent his anger upon them. 25 So Moses went down to the people and told them lest He make a breach against them.*

PREPARING FOR THE COVENANT

G-d had promised Abraham that He would make a covenant with his descendants. Jacob, the grandson of Abraham, together with all his family went down to Egypt to escape the ravages of famine. G-d changed Jacob's name to Israel and, according to the chronology of the Torah, by the time they left Egypt 210 years later, they had grown into a nation of 600,000 men.

49 days after leaving Egypt, G-d kept His word to Abraham by entering into a covenant with the Israelites at Mount Sinai. This chapter describes the preparations that took place in the days leading up to what is believed by Jews to be the defining event of Judaism: when G-d spoke to the entire nation.

THE RELATIONSHIP BETWEEN G-D AND ISRAEL

The Midrash compares this covenant to a wedding. G-d is the bridegroom, Israel is the bride, Mount Sinai is the chuppah (wedding canopy), the Torah is the ketubah (marriage contract) and tefillin is the ring. The relationship between G-d and Israel is therefore to be compared to the relationship between a husband and wife:

Just as:	G-d provides Israel with all its material needs
So must:	a husband must provide his wife with all her material needs
0	Israel must be loyal to G-d and not worship idols/embrace other religions
So must:	a wife be loyal and faithful to her husband
Just as:	two people marry primarily because they love each other
So must:	Israel commit to G-d because they love Him, knowing He commits to them because He loves them
Just as:	the ketubah lists a husband's obligations towards his wife
So does:	the Torah list G-d's commitment to provide for Israel

<u>Note:</u> Although the Torah appears to contain a list of Israel's obligations to G-d [the 613 commandments] these are in fact considered secondary to the assurances the Torah gives that, if Israel are loyal to G-d, all their needs will be provided.

Finally, Jewish law requires a husband to seal the marriage by presenting his wife with something of unambiguous monetary value under the chuppah. The universal custom is to use a ring. This symbolises his commitment to provide for his wife and serves as a token of his love for her. Similarly, every morning, before going to his work, a man puts on tefillin to remind himself of G-d's love for Israel and His commitment to provide all their needs.

WHY WAS THERE A NEED FOR PREPARATION?

The Midrash[74] gives two explanations. It compares the Israelites, when they left Egypt, to an invalid who needs a period of convalescence after a serious illness. Their new-found freedom from slavery was something with which it would take them time to become familiar. It also highlights their need for time to appreciate G-d's love for them:

> There was once a prince who sought a wife. He met a very beautiful girl from an eminent family and realised she was what he was looking for. In order to impress her with his love and devotion, he showered her with gifts. When she visited the bakery, he ordered an enormous cream cake be specially prepared for her; she visited a clothes store and he ordered the finest dress be made for her; she went to the jewellers and he ordered the finest diamonds for her.

The prince is G-d who showered Israel with gifts before the covenant was entered at Mount Sinai. In order to release them from Egyptian bondage He brought the ten plagues on the Egyptians. When they were pursued by Egypt, He split the Red Sea for them. He saved them from an Amalekite attack, provided them with manna to eat and a well for water. Only after providing all these 'gifts' did the revelation at Sinai take place.

THE UNITY OF THE PEOPLE

The commentaries point out that when it says: Israel encamped opposite the mountain, the verb encamped is written in Hebrew in the singular [vayichan – and he encamped instead of vayachanu – and they encamped]. They explain this to be a hint at the unity of the people at this time. They encamped, as it were, as one person. Despite their disagreements and different points of view, they put all that behind them and committed themselves to each other first in order to commit themselves together to enter G-d's covenant. Some learn from here that the removal of dissension and strife among ourselves is an essential pre-requisite to a relationship with G-d.

WE WILL DO AND WE WILL HEAR

When Moses told the people that G-d would make a covenant with them, they replied: All which G-d has spoken, we will do. This is means that the Israelites committed themselves to G-d's covenant without knowing what it was that G-d required of them. They agreed to obey the laws of the Torah without knowing what they were. This does not mean that they blindly, irrationally agreed to do whatever they were told. On the contrary, their response is considered by Jewish tradition to be the highest level of Divine worship. They possessed an absolute certainty of G-d's existence and love for them. They had no doubt that whatever He commanded them would be an expression of that love and that obeying His commandments would always be for their benefit.

---

74   *Yalkut Shimoni I #272*

At the end of the covenant narrative, when Moses had finished speaking, the people respond: all which G-d has spoken we will do and we will hear.[75] This indicates a further commitment. *It is impossible to observe G-d's commandments properly unless one understands them.* A commitment to study the Torah constantly is implied here. There is a famous Talmudic statement that the study of the Torah is equal to the observance of all the commandments.[76]

---

75   *Exodus 24:7*
76   *TB Shabbat 127a*

COVENANT WITH MOSES - 2
Exodus 20

1 And G-d spoke all these words saying. 2 I am the Lord your G-d who brought you out from the land of Egypt from the house of slavery. 3 There will not be for you any other gods besides Me. 4 Do not make for yourselves a graven image or any picture of that which is in the heavens above or which is on the earth below or which is in the water beneath the earth. 5 Do not bow down to them and do not worship them for I, the Lord your G-d, am a zealous G-d who visits the sin of the fathers upon the children, upon the third and upon the fourth [generation] of those who hate Me. 6 But does kindness to thousands [of generations] to those who love Me and keep My commandments.

7 Do not take the Name of the Lord your G-d in vain for G-d will not acquit those who take His Name in vain.

8 Remember the Sabbath day to sanctify it. 9 Six days you shall labour and do all your work. 10 But the seventh day is Shabbat to the Lord your G-d; you shall not do any work, you or your son or your daughter, your servant or your maidservant or your animals or your stranger within your gates. 11 For in six days G-d made the heavens and the earth, the sea and all which is in them and He rested on the seventh day; therefore G-d blessed the Shabbat day and He sanctified it.

12 Honour your father and your mother in order that your days be long upon the earth which the Lord your G-d is giving you.

13 You shall not murder;   you shall not commit adultery;   you shall not steal;   you shall not be a false witness against your fellow. 14 You shall not covet your neighbour's house;   you shall not covet your neighbour's wife or his servant or his maidservant or his ox or his donkey or anything which [belongs] to your neighbour.

15 And all the people could see the sounds and the flames and the sound of the shofar and the mountain smoking; and the people saw and they trembled and they stood from afar. 16 And they said to Moses: you speak with us and we will listen, let G-d not speak with us lest we die. 17 And Moses said to the people: do not be afraid for [it is] in order to exalt you that G-d has come and in order that the fear of Him be before you so that you shall not sin. 18 So the people stood from afar and Moses approached the mist [within which] G-d was there. 19 Then G-d said to Moses: thus shall you say to the all children of Israel: you have seen that from the heavens I have spoken with you. 20 Do not make [alongside] Me gods of silver or gods of gold: you shall not make [them] for yourselves. 21 An altar of earth you shall make for Me and you shall slaughter upon it your burnt offerings and your peace offerings, your flock and you're herd: in every place where I shall mention My Name I shall come to you and I shall bless you. 22And when you make an altar of stones for Me do not build them hewn lest you wave your sword upon it and defile it. 23 And do not ascend by steps upon My altar that your nakedness be not uncovered upon it.

THE TEN COMMANDMENTS

Unlike the seven Noahide laws, which provide a structure for people to live harmoniously together, the Ten Commandments *define the relationship between G-d and Israel.* Even though the last five commandments concern laws between man and his neighbour that is because the way one Jew relates to another Jew is determined by G-d's instructions.

The Ten Commandments can be understood sequentially, the first being a pre-requisite for the second, which is a pre-requisite for the observance of the third, and so on. In this way, *the Ten Commandments provide the 'building blocks' for each Jew to develop a relationship with G-d* through which it will be possible to emulate Abraham and become the kind of person able to fulfil G-'s covenant.

#1 - KNOW THERE IS A G-D

Moses Maimonides, in his codification of the 613 commandments in the Torah, listed this as the very first commandment.[77] The Torah states that G-d spoke from Mount Sinai and every single Jew heard Him. Before they were given the Torah, they were provided with total certainty that G-d did exist and that He was giving them the Torah. In the same way, *every Jew is required to achieve a certainty in their own mind that G-d exists* and that He gave the Torah to the Jewish people.

It is not important how one achieves this certainty. Some will engage in philosophical speculation, considering the 'evidence' in nature, in history or in logic. Others will be influenced by personal experience of His providence. Some might even consider it so obvious that no thought about it is even necessary!

#2 – DO NOT WORSHIP IDOLS

Knowing that G-d exists does not preclude the possibility of there being many forces in the universe. This is what was assumed in the ancient world. They believed that there were competing supernatural forces that were in a constant state of conflict. The nation who aligned itself to the stronger god would always prevail. Humanity, therefore, was forever plagued by the dilemma of trying to know which force (idol) to worship. Nations defeated in battle would routinely ascribe blame for their defeat on the superiority of the idol of their enemies. They would consequently reject and discard their (defeated) idols and adopt the worship of the idols of their conquerors.

This commandment emphasises that *all forces in the universe are controlled by G-d.* Any belief that something is somehow independent of and not under the control of G-d is a form of idolatry.

---

77   *Mishneh Torah: Foundations of Belief 1:1*

Some say there is still a form of idolatry around today. The ancients may have worshipped the forces of nature but modern 'idolaters' worship the forces of economics, politics, science and, perhaps most of all, money.

The starting point of Judaism consequently is first to satisfy oneself that G-d does exist and then that He alone controls the entire universe. This gives one the security and peace-of-mind to know that *there are no 'coincidences' or 'bad luck'.* Everything is part of the Divine plan and, of course, the Divine Planner is our Father in heaven who loves us and so we can accept whatever happens to us in life as being 'for the best'.

#3 – DO NOT BLASPHEME/TAKE G-D'S NAME IN VAIN

Having established the reality of G-d's existence and the extent of His power now follows the instruction on *how to develop a relationship with G-d.* This command directs Israel on how to live with a consciousness of the greatness of G-d.

It is considered disrespectful to refer to a parent or authority figure (or one significantly older than oneself) by their first name since such *over-familiarity suggests a form of equality.* Similarly, to refer to G-d by His Name at any time is considered inappropriate. On one occasion in the year, on Yom Kippur, the holiest day of the year, in the holiest place on earth, the Temple, the holiest man on earth, the High Priest, would pronounce this Name and all the people would prostrate themselves on the floor when they heard it. This ceremony is recalled yearly by Orthodox Jews in the Mussaf service on Yom Kippur.

The Talmud debates whether it was the tetragrammaton [4-letter Name written but not pronounced in siddurim] or the 72-letter Name that is forbidden to be pronounced. The tradition has now been lost as to how either of those Names are to be pronounced. *Orthodox Jews avoid using any Name of G-d at all,* except in prayer. In speech, they say HaShem [literally the Name] and when writing they replace the 'o' with a hyphen.

This acknowledgement of G-d's superiority over human beings has two main benefits. Firstly, it promotes *humility* with a realisation of one's own limitations. Secondly, when responding positively to this realisation, it *encourages personal growth* and development. Similarly, when one has a healthy consciousness of one's own limitations, this leads one to have *respect for others* who have reached greater levels and a positive desire to emulate them.

#4 – REMEMBER/KEEP THE SABBATH DAY

Once an appropriate relationship with G-d has been established, Israel must now begin to *live and act in accordance with His requirements.* The Talmud explains that the Shabbat laws actually govern all seven days of the week. The Mishnah[78] lists 39 prohibited categories of work.

---

78   *Shabbat 7:2*

The Talmud explains that these 39 activities were the very labours required for the building of the Mishkan, the portable tabernacle used by the Israelites as the centre of worship until the Temple was built. G-d instructed Israel to build the Mishkan so that *I may dwell in their midst*.[79]

Why doesn't it say: *that I may dwell in it*? The Talmud explains that there is a deeper message in this instruction. For six days of the week, Jews are instructed to build a Mishkan, i.e. make their work and home environment, as it were, conducive to G-d's presence. This is achieved by *having responsibility in supporting one's family, acting honestly in business, showing care and consideration for others* in social situations and compassion for those in need. It is also achieved by utilising all one's time appropriately, for example, setting aside time to study Torah and not frivolously wasting one's free time from one Shabbat to the next. The first 'law' of Shabbat, consequently is: *six days you shall labour*[80].

For six days, Jews are instructed to *make the world the place G-d would want it to be*. This is the practical fulfilment of the covenant. On the seventh day, however, every week, they are to take a step back and remind themselves that, even though G-d has given Israel responsibility for His world, nevertheless the world does not belong to them. Also, despite all their efforts and accomplishments, they are to remember that no success is possible without G-d's assistance and support. Shabbat, consequently, is Israel's weekly 'reality check'!

#5 - HONOUR YOUR FATHER AND YOUR MOTHER

Since this command appears on the first tablet, it is understood as *a command between man and G-d*. Why is this? When a baby is born, it is completely dependant upon its parents who, in normal circumstances, provide the baby's every material and emotional because of their love and strong desire for their child to have the best of everything. In the same way, Israel are to understand that *G-d is their Father* in heaven who provides them with all their needs in His abounding love for them.

Just as a loving parent will establish rules and impose discipline for the benefit of their children, so also G-d establishes rules [the 613 commandments in the Torah] and disciplines [punishes] Israel when they go astray in order to guide them in the ways that ultimately will be the most beneficial for them. *Parents, consequently, have the responsibility of being role models* for their children in how to form and develop a relationship with G-d.

---

79   *Exodus 25:8*
80   *Ibid. 20:9*

This commandment represents the 'starting point' for every Jew to develop a relationship with G-d. If parents provide the correct home environment, their children will grow up with feelings of trust and security that their parents are always there when they need them. As adults, this trust and security will transfer to G-d.

The Rabbis have enacted numerous laws for the purpose of establishing the correct relationship between parents and children in the spirit of this commandment. For example, it is forbidden in Jewish law to contradict one's parents in public, to raise one's voice to a parent at any time or to sit in their particular seat. Many would apply these laws to their relationship with their Rabbi. *Although this is the last of the 'man and G-d' commandments, it is also the link to the 'man and his neighbour' commandments.* In normal circumstances, the parent-child relationship is unique. Only parents accept and love you unconditionally just because you are you. Only parents continue to provide for you asking nothing in return.

If someone cannot appreciate the kindness done for them by their parents, it will be virtually impossible for them to appreciate the goodness in and form healthy relationships with people of their own age.

Psychologists have shown that there is a consistent link between those who come from an unhappy home background and those who have difficulty forming social relationships. The purpose of this commandment, consequently, is also to provide the potential for an individual to be able to relate healthily with others. How this is to be accomplished is explained in the second half of the Ten Commandments.

#6 – DO NOT MURDER

Murder is the most extreme physical damage that one human being can inflict upon another human being. It is also irreversible. However 'sorry' a murderer may be, he cannot bring his victim back to life! This prohibition, consequently, begins the process of appreciating both the value and the needs of another human being.

Murder is the ultimate act of selfishness. It says: my needs/desires come before somebody else's right to live. A baby only identifies its own desires. Learning to relate to others begins by recognising the need to remove this trait of selfishness. The first stage is to appreciate that other people must be taken into consideration sometimes.

On a deeper level, *murder is also a crime against G-d.* G-d decides when it is time for somebody to leave this world. For someone to, as it were, take this law into their own hands is to rebel against G-d's plan for the world. Of course, there are occasions when the Torah permits the killing of another human being: a court may execute those found guilty of capital crimes; war may be waged against one's enemies in certain circumstances. That is why the command is do not murder (which is taking life contrary to G-d's will) not do not kill, because sometimes G-d wishes/allows us to terminate life.

There is a Talmudic principle that every negative commandment contains an implied positive commandment as well. Since murder is the removal of a person from their physical environment, any action which helps to bring a person into their physical environment would be the negation of murder. *From here it is deduced that it is meritorious to make newcomers welcome, to assist those who are shy and to avoid anything which would embarrass someone else, for embarrassment makes a person want to leave their environment.*

#7– DO NOT COMMIT ADULTERY

In Jewish tradition, marriage is viewed as the spiritual completion of a human being (see Covenant with Adam: Male and Female for details). Adultery, consequently, which destroys a marriage, is considered a form of *spiritual murder*, it is the murder of the image of G-d that is completed with the union of a man and a woman. Like murder, adultery is also irreversible, for one who commits adultery is forbidden in Torah law to remain married to their partner. It is also an extreme manifestation of selfishness, for the adulterers put the need to satisfy their desires before any consideration for the hurt and damage this would do to their marriage partner or to the children of that marriage.

All physical relationships outside marriage are forbidden in Torah law, but adultery has the most serious consequences. In order to distance a person from this transgression, the Rabbis have constructed a body of laws of moral and modest conduct which are today a significant and identifiable feature of Orthodox Jewish life:

Rabbinic law *forbids any physical contact* between men and women outside the immediate family;

A man and a woman *may not be alone* in a secluded area;

Modesty in dress is essential in all public activities;

Married women must *cover their hair* in public.

Social contact between the sexes is minimised. Social events are often characterised by the *mechitzah,* a solid partition between the men and the women. Most Orthodox Jews will send their children to single sex schools and encourage social activities such as outings, holidays and camps to be in a single sex environment.

#8 – DO NOT STEAL

This commandment has been traditionally understood as a prohibition against kidnapping.[81] The essence of the human condition is to have free-will. The act of kidnapping takes away a person's ability to exercise that free-will and reduces their existence to the status of an animal. Kidnapping, consequently, is seen as *the removal of the humanity from the human being.*

---

81   *TB Sanhedrin 86a (quoted by Rashi: Exodus 20:13)*

Any act which forces others to do that which, if they used their free-will they would not do, is forbidden. Religious cults or unscrupulous charismatic leaders who brainwash others to follow them violate this commandment. A free society is one in which thinking or expressing one's own opinion, no matter how controversial, is actively encouraged. All the great works of Torah scholarship, from the Talmud to the present day, are replete with controversy and diversity of opinion. The law follows the majority view, but all opinions are freely expressed, respected and recorded for future generations.

Lesser forms of theft are also included in this commandment. *Stealing is also a manifestation of selfishness.* It says: my needs/desires come before other people's possessions. The Torah requires a thief to repay double what he stole. The exact amount by which he plotted to dishonestly profit is the amount by which he must lose. The punishment of the thief, consequently, teaches him the lesson he most needs to learn, i.e. what it is like to have taken from you the very amount that he sought to steal.

Stealing does not just involve possessions. *One can steal time, by wasting the time of others.* One can steal a person's privacy by prying into things which are not intended for public knowledge. Some might conclude that many of the practices of investigative journalism would be prohibited by this commandment. One can steal a person's good name by spreading false rumours about them.

#9 – DO NOT BE A FALSE WITNESS

The first three commandments of the second 'tablet' are concerned with individual relationships, i.e. how people relate to each other on an individual level. The final two commandments are concerned with the *organisation of society* as a whole.

It is impossible for any society to function efficiently if there is not a general respect for its institutions from the majority of its citizens. The most essential social institutions of all are those which ensure that society has a system of justice: the government that makes the laws; the police that enforce the laws; and the courts that deal with those accused of breaking the laws. Why is this so important?

If people do not basically trust the government to make sensible laws, the police to protect them and the courts to see that justice is done then nobody will feel safe. Lawlessness will soon take control and society will no longer be able to function.

Witnesses are the most important element of this whole system. If witnesses cannot be relied upon to come forward when they have testimony to give (and to tell the truth when they give their testimony) then the courts will not be able to convict criminals, the police will be unable to do their job and the laws passed by the government will have no meaning. Criminals will become bolder and more ruthless and law-abiding citizens will live in constant fear of becoming the victim of a crime.

The commandment not to be a false witness is about much more than being an honest person who always tells the truth. It is the pre-requisite to having a just society in which its honest citizens can live in peace and security.

#10 – DO NOT BE JEALOUS

Whilst it is obvious that jealousy is a bad character trait, that alone would be an insufficient reason to include it in the Ten Commandments. In fact, *jealousy undermines the whole fabric of society*. When people cannot tolerate the fact that someone else has something that they don't have or that they can't have, then it becomes impossible for a society to function in a spirit of harmony and co-operation.

Just as 'honour your father and your mother' is the starting-point to developing a relationship with G-d so *jealousy is the starting-point for breaking all the commandments concerning other people*. Once jealousy takes over, one will be prepared to tell lies, to steal, to commit adultery and ultimately even to murder if that is what it takes to remove the feeling of jealousy.

Jealousy is a also a denial of G-d. It is impossible to believe that G-d provides for the needs of all fairly and at the same time to be jealous of what someone else possesses. In this way, the last of the Ten Commandments links back to the first. The opposite of being jealous is being happy with one's portion. One can only be truly happy with what one has if one truly believes that this is what one should have. It is impossible to believe this (for there are always plenty of things that one does not have or cannot afford) without a belief that G-d provides everybody with all their needs. *In order to completely eliminate jealousy, consequently, one needs to know there is a G-d, which is where the Ten Commandments began!*

COVENANT WITH MOSES - 3
Exodus 21-24

After recording the Ten Commandments, the Torah then lists (in Chapters 21-23) a series of social laws which provide the legal framework for communal Jewish life. Chapter 24 then describes how the covenant at Mount Sinai was concluded.

The Midrash[82] concludes, however, that this is not a chronological sequence. Some of these social laws were already taught to the people before the revelation at Mount Sinai and others are only introduced here and further details follow later in the Torah. The fact that the Torah puts these social laws between the commencement and conclusion of the covenant event, however, is very significant.

These laws follow on immediately after the narrative of the Ten Commandments to emphasise the importance of social harmony and personal responsibility. Living peacefully, respecting the needs and possessions of others and showing due consideration are not just optional ethical standards. They are essential elements in the Sinai covenant. Israel's commitment to G-d was as much a commitment to care for each other as it was a commitment to follow G-d's laws.

Hirsch[83] points out that this legal narrative begins with laws pertaining to the treatment of slaves, the destitute and the criminal. He sees in this an instruction that a Jewish society must make the needs of the least fortunate their first priority.

This principle is further emphasised by the responsibility placed on the courts to pursue justice:

> ...you shall not pervert justice [against] the poor... distance yourself from a false word; do not put to death one who is innocent... do not take a bribe [or] oppress the stranger... for you were strangers in the land of Egypt.[84]

All people need to feel equally responsibility to uphold the law. The integrity of the courts is essential if people are to have confidence in its authority.

The Torah encourages individuals to take responsibility for their actions when they have done wrong. A thief who admits his guilt need only repay what he stole, but if he dishonestly protests his innocence and is later found guilty by the court he must repay double.[85] The opening verses of Chapter 22 explain the different levels of liability for those who borrow or hire property from others and damage them.

---

82   *Shemot Rabba 30:8*
83   *Rabbi Samson Raphael Hirsch: Commentary on the Pentateuch: Exodus 21:1*
84   *Exodus 21:6-9*
85   *Exodus 22:3*

Individuals are also encouraged to take responsibility for that which is damaged by their property. The Torah requires compensation being paid for damage done by one's animals,[86] by an obstacle one left in a public place[87] or by a fire that spreads from one's property.[88] These laws are analysed in great depth in the Talmud and have become the standard Talmud syllabus of most Orthodox Jewish schools and Yeshivot.

After the failure of the world to live according to the covenant with Adam, it was replaced by the covenant with Noah, which remains to this day the prescription for a righteous life for all the non-Jewish nations. G-d then made an exclusive covenant with Abraham, the terms of which were defined by the covenant made at Mount Sinai. From this point on, *it was now Israel's responsibility to lead the world towards the purpose for which it was originally created.* This they would do by observing the commandments of the Torah and, by emphasising the social laws, being the role model example to all nations of the characteristics of honesty, compassion and sensitivity to the needs of others.

---

86   *Exodus 21:28-32*
87   *Exodus 21:33-34*
88   *Exodus 22:5*

COVENANT WITH DAVID
II Samuel 7

1 And it was when the king dwelt in his house and G-d had given him rest all around from his enemies. 2 Then the king said to Nathan the prophet: see now; I am dwelling in a house of cedars and the Ark of G-d is dwelling [only] within the curtain. 3 And Nathan said to the king: all which is in your heart go [and] do for G-d is with you. 4 And it was on that [very night] the word of G-d [came] to Nathan saying. 5 Go; and say to My servant, to David [that] so said G-d: shall you build a house for Me for My dwelling? 6 For I have not dwelt in a house from the day that I brought up the children of Israel from Egypt until this day but I have moved around in a tent and a tabernacle. 7 In all [places] where I have moved around amongst all the children of Israel did I [ever] speak a word to [even] one of the leaders of Israel whom I commanded to shepherd My people saying: why have you not built for Me a house of cedars? 8 And now, so shall you say to My servant, to David [that] so said the Lord of Hosts: I have selected [lit: taken] you from the flock from following the sheep to be a leader over My people, over Israel. 9 And I have been with you wherever you have gone and I have cut off all your enemies from before you and I have made you a great name like the name of [previous] great ones in the world. 10 And I will assign a place for My people, for Israel and I will plant them [firmly] and [they] shall dwell under [its protection] and [they] shall not be made nervous any more and wicked ones will no longer continue to afflict them. 11 And [even] from the day on which I commanded judges [to rule] over My people Israel; and I shall give you rest from all your enemies: and G-d has told you that G-d will make a house for you. 12 When your days will be filled and you lie with your fathers then I will raise up your son [lit: seed] after you, [one] who will go out from your loins and I will establish his kingdom. 13 He will build a house for My Name and I will establish the throne of his kingdom forever. 14 I will be to him as a father and he will be to Me as a son who, when he goes astray, I will chastise him with the rod of men and with the plagues of people. 15 But My kindness shall not depart from him as I withdrew it from Saul whom I removed from before you.

16 But your house and your kingdom will be made firm before you forever; your throne will be set firm for ever. 17 According to all these words and all this vision, so did Nathan speak to David. 18 Then King David came and sat before G-d and said: who am I O Lord G-d and what [importance] is my house that You have brought me so far? 19 And even this appears insignificant in Your eyes O Lord G-d that You have spoken also [of] your servant's house in the distant [future]; yet this is the treatment [lit: law] of a [great] man O Lord G-d. 20 And what more can David speak to You for You know Your servant O Lord G-d. 21 For the sake of Your word and according to Your heart You have done all this greatness to make [it] known to Your servant. 22 Therefore are You [alone] great O Lord G-d and there are no gods besides You just as we have heard with our ears. 23 And who are like Your people, like Israel, a unique nation in the world, that G-d went to redeem for Himself for a people, to establish a Name for Himself and to do for You the great and awesome [deeds] for Your land for the sake of Your people who You redeemed for Yourself from Egypt [driving out each] nation and its god? 24 And You established Your people Israel for Yourself as a people forever, and You, G-d have become their G-d. 25 And now O Lord G-d, the matter of which You have spoken concerning Your servant, concerning his house: let it be established forever and do as You have spoken. 26 And may Your Name be exalted forever that [people may] say: the Lord of Hosts is G-d over Israel and the house of Your servant David is made firm forever. 27 For You Lord of Hosts, G-d of Israel have revealed [it in] Your servant's ear saying: a house I shall build for you; therefore Your servant has found [in] his heart to pray to You [the words of] this prayer. 28 And now O Lord G-d, You [alone] are G-d and Your words [will come] true [as] You have spoken to Your servant [of all] this goodness. 29 And now let it please [You] to bless the house of Your servant to be forever before You, for You O Lord G-d have spoken [it] and through Your blessing let Your servant's house be blessed forever.

KING DAVID WISHES TO BUILD A HOUSE FOR G-D

We may well wonder why King David wanted to build a house for G-d at just this moment. In order to understand this, we have to link this narrative to the covenant G-d made with Israel at Mount Sinai.

When the Israelites finally left the wilderness and entered the land under the leadership of Joshua, they had been commanded to conquer the land in its entirety and completely *drive out the seven Canaanite nations* living there. The Torah says that, when this has been accomplished and *peace has been established,* then they may *appoint a king.*[89] It is then the king's responsibility to *build the Temple*, the house of G-d, and lead Israel towards the fulfillment of the Sinai covenant.

Unfortunately, this is not what actually happened. In *the book of Joshua*, we see that the Israelites did not drive out all of the Canaanites, but allowed some of them to remain. As a consequence of this, we see in *the book of Judges* that they were constantly troubled by attacks from the surrounding nations, usually aided and abetted by the Canaanites. This culminated, in *the first book of Samuel* by the people despairing of their inability to maintain peace and demanding that Samuel ... set up for us a king to judge us like all the nations[90].

The Talmud states that the people wanted a king so they could be like all the nations. This was their mistakes. *They did not need a king to lead them into battle and fight their wars for they had G-d to do that for them.* Israel's king had a different function, as will be explained. That is why, although G-d acceded to their request, they were only granted a temporary king, King Saul. [91]

Even when David became king at the beginning of *the second book of Samuel,* it was still not yet the right time for a king. First, King David had to subdue all the surrounding nations and bring peace to the land. When this had been achieved, King David realized that now he could really be the king that G-d had originally instructed the people to appoint and, therefore, now was the time to build the Temple.

KING DAVID IS TOLD NOT TO BUILD THE HOUSE

It is clear from the narrative that King David was right to suggest that he should now build the Temple. Even Nathan, the greatest prophet of the generation, told him to go ahead. That is why G-d had to come to Nathan that night to tell him to warn King David that G-d did not want him to build the Temple. Why wasn't David allowed to build the Temple?

---

89   *Deuteronomy 18:14-15*
90   *I Samuel 8:5*
91   *TB Sanhedrin 20b*

Just before he dies, King David says to his son Solomon:

> [G-d said to me] you shall not build a house for My Name for much blood have you spilled on the ground before Me...[92]

Rabbi Yehudah Leib Ginzberg[93] points that there is no indication here that King David had done anything wrong. Rather, *it was inappropriate that a Temple of peace be built by a man of war*. The Midrash, however, indicates a more subtle reason for not letting King David build the Temple:

> *After being told he was not to build the Temple, King David said:* I am obviously considered unfit to build the Holy Temple.
> *To this G-d replied:* [I swear] by your life that all the blood that you have shed has brought no more guilt upon you than shedding the blood of the ram and the deer.
> *King David then asked:* Master of the Universe, if that is so then why can I not build it?
> *G-d answered:* It is known before Me that the Israelites in the future shall sin. I will then be able to expend My anger upon My Temple so that they shall be spared. But if you were to build the Temple, then it could never be destroyed.[94]

According to this idea, *King David was too great to build the Temple*. His greatness was such that G-d entered into a covenant with him to establish a permanent royal dynasty with him and his descendants. If not for the sins of the people, the establishment of the monarchy and building of the Temple would have led to the commencement of the Messianic Age. Instead, the Messianic Age would have to be postponed until some future, unspecified time. The Temple would therefore be a building of lesser spiritual perfection built by his son.

When Israel will have finally atoned for her sins, the monarchy will be restored through a descendant of King David who will build the final permanent Temple and the Mesianic Age will then begin.

G-D PROMISES TO MAKE KING DAVID A HOUSE

Even though G-d did not allow King David to build the Temple that does not mean that he was in some way rejected by G-d. On the contrary, G-d's response was to tell Nathan that He would build a house for King David!

The covenant G-d made with King David was similar to the one He made with Abraham. G-d made a covenant with Abraham in which his descendants would be role models to all the rest of the world of how G-d wants people to live. Similarly, G-d made a covenant with King David in which his descendants would be role models to Israel of the concept of majesty in human form, as will be explained.

---

92   *I Chronicles 22:6-8*
93   *Mussar HeNeiyim: Shmuel [a modern commentary on Prophets]*
94   *Tehillim Rabba 2; a similar idea is found in Tosephos: Kiddushin 31b*

By entering into a covenant with King David and his descendants, G-d confirms that his family alone is to be considered Israel's rightful king. The covenant also indicates that the prophecy given to Jacob that the sceptre shall not depart from Judah[95] was to be fulfilled only through King David (who was from the tribe of Judah) and his descendants. It does not mean that there will be an uninterrupted rule for, as G-d points out (vv. 14-15) if the kings failed to fulfill their side of the covenant their authority could be removed. Rather, it means that nobody else can claim to be Israel's rightful king. Eventually, Israel was sent into exile to live without a king. It is a fundamental Jewish belief, however, that the kingdom of David will be restored in the Messianic era. In Jewish literature, the Messiah is often referred to as Mashiach ben David, the Messiah, son [i.e. descendant] of David.

KING DAVID'S RESPONSE TO G-D'S PROMISE

King David responds to G-d's promise in three ways: he expresses humility and his unworthiness for such an honour; he praises G-d who is Israel's real king; he praises Israel as G-d's chosen people. From this response, the Talmud understands the role of a Jewish king:

SPIRITUAL LEADER

Even before G-d made the covenant with him, King David wanted to build the Temple, the spiritual focal point of Jewish worship. Even though King David did not build it, his son King Solomon did, confirming that it was the responsibility of the king to build the Temple. The first responsibility of the king, consequently, is the spiritual welfare of the people.

THE CONCEPT OF MAJESTY IN HUMAN FORM

In his humility, King David recognises that G-d is the real king of Israel, He is merely a human representation of G-d's majesty. How does this work?

G-d is an absolute power who must be obeyed. One can expect to be punished if G-d's laws are broken. If G-d decides to punish, no power in the universe can withstand Him. At the same time, G-d only punishes out of love for His creations, that they be encouraged to improve themselves. In the same way, a human king must be granted absolute authority over his subjects but must use that authority to deal justly with his people. Even when harshness is required, it must not be for his own benefit but with the best interests of the people as a whole in mind. In this way, a righteous king represents the concept of majesty in human form, whilst reminding himself and his subjects that true majesty belongs to G-d alone.

---

95   *Genesis 49:10*

In order to maintain the king's humility, the Torah commands him to write his own Sefer Torah that must accompany him wherever he goes. In order to maintain this majestic image, the Mishnah states that the king's hair must be cut daily and he must always wear royal robes in public. There is a special blessing to be recited when one sees the king, none may sit in his presence or turn their back on him[96]

DOES G-D SHOW FAVOURITISM TO KING DAVID?

The Talmud[97] asks why it was that King Saul committed but one sin (the failure to wipe out Amalek) and had the kingdom taken away from him, yet King David committed many sins and did not have the kingdom taken away from him. Why is G-d biased in King David's favour?

The Talmud explains that it is not really a bias at all. From the days of Jacob, it was known that, when the time came to appoint Israel's rightful king, he would be from the tribe of Judah. When the people demanded that Samuel anoint for them a king, it was the wrong time and for the wrong reasons. Nevertheless, G-d permitted a temporary arrangement. Saul was therefore chosen to be a temporary king, not a permanent king. King Saul was not even from the tribe of Judah. He was a Benjaminite. As such, he could only remain king so long as he did not sin.

King David, on the other hand, was chosen to be a permanent king and to establish the covenant of majesty for all time. When he sinned, therefore, he was punished in other ways but did not have the throne taken away from him. This does not mean that King Saul was discriminated against. On the contrary, the Talmud concludes that ...were you Saul and he David I should have destroyed many David's before him...In some ways, King Saul as an individual was more righteous than King David. It is just that he was not the legitimate king of Israel.

There is another point which demonstrates that bias was not shown in King David's favour. As we have seen, King David was not permitted to build the Temple. Just as King Saul was not the person to establish Israel's monarchy, so King David was not the person to build Israel's Temple.

---

96   *Sanhedrin 2:2-5*
97   *TB Horayot 11b*

COVENANT WITH JEREMIAH
Jeremiah 31:30-39

30 *Behold days are coming says the Lord when I will form a covenant with the house of Israel and the house of Judah, a new covenant.* 31 *Not like the covenant that I formed with their forefathers on the day I took them by the hand to take them out of the land of Egypt, for they broke My covenant although I was Lord over them, says the Lord.* 32 *For this is the covenant I will form with the house of Israel after those days, says the Lord: I will place My Torah in their midst and I will inscribe it upon their hearts and I will be their G-d and they will be My people.* 33 *And no longer shall one teach his neighbour or one his brother saying: know the Lord; for they shall all know Me from their smallest to their greatest, says the Lord, for I will forgive their iniquity and their sin I will no longer remember.* 34 *So said the Lord who gives the sun to illuminate the day, the laws of the moon to illuminate the night, who stirs up the sea and its waves roar, the Lord of Hosts is His Name.* 35 *If these laws depart from before Me, says the Lord, so will the seed of Israel cease being a nation before Me for all time.* 36 *So said the Lord: if the heavens above will be measured and the foundations of the earth below will be fathomed, I too will reject all the seed of Israel because of all they did, says the Lord.* 37 *Behold days are coming, says the Lord, when the city shall be built to the Lord from the tower of Hananel until the gate of the corner.* 38 *And the measuring line shall go out further opposite it upon the hill of Gareb and it shall turn to Goah.* 39 *And the whole valley of the dead bodies and the ash and all the fields until the Kidron valley until the corner of the Horse Gate to the east shall be holy to the Lord; it shall never again be uprooted or torn down.*

THE NEW COVENANT

Why did G-d find it necessary to make a new covenant? In order to understand this, we have to link this prophecy to the covenant G-d made with King David. King David was promised that a permanent kingdom would now be established with his descendants. His son, King Solomon, succeeded him and built the Temple. At that point, Israel had the opportunity to fulfill the covenant made at Sinai and lead the world to completion. Unfortunately, they did not do this.

In the days of King Rehoboam, the son of King Solomon, the kingdom split in two and the ten northern tribes formed a new kingdom, leaving only the tribes of Judah and Benjamin under the authority of the Davidic king. The two books of Kings record how both kingdoms degenerated until the Assyrians conquered and exiled the ten tribes, leaving only the southern kingdom of Judea. Approximately a hundred years after the Assyrian conquest of the northern kingdom, the Babylonians had risen to become the dominant empire. Eventually, they conquered and exiled the southern kingdom and destroyed the First Temple. The prophecy of the new covenant was given in the period immediately before the Babylonian conquest and destruction of the Temple.

Jeremiah lived at the time of the destruction of the First Temple. Most of his prophecies included harsh condemnations of the people's conduct, combined with warnings of the imminent conquest and exile of the people and destruction of the Temple. Interspersed with these rebukes, however, were prophecies of consolation for the post-destruction era. The prophecy of the new covenant is one of these prophecies of consolation.

Jeremiah received a message from G-d saying that, in days to come, He will enter into a 'new covenant' with Israel, unlike the one He made with them at Mount Sinai. Christians and Jews have a very different understanding of what this means.

CHRISTIAN INTERPRETATION

According to the Christians, this was a prophecy of Israel's rejection. Israel had been denounced by all the prophets for violating the covenant made at Mount Sinai and failing to properly observe the commandments of the Torah. G-d's patience with them would eventually be exhausted and He would banish them into exile and terminate their status as the Chosen People. He would then establish a new covenant in which the observance of the laws of the Torah was no longer required.

The fulfilment of this prophecy was realised with the appearance of the Christian Messiah (believed to be a descendant of King David) and the terms of this covenant are to be found in the New Testament (The name 'New Testament' is actually derived from the Christian interpretation of the new covenant.) All those who follow the Christian messiah become the new 'Israel' and belief in him guarantees salvation in the world to come.

JEWISH INTERPRETATION

According to the Jewish interpretation, Jeremiah is prophesising about a time far in the future, referred to in the Talmud as the end of days. Israel was to be banished into exile for failing to keep the covenant made at Mount Sinai, but they would remain the Chosen People. The exile and persecution that they would endure would be their punishment. The time will come, however, when the punishment is completed and, at that time, G-d will renew His covenant with His people. Since Israel had failed to keep the Sinai covenant, G-d will have to enter into a new covenant with Israel in which Israel will again pledge themselves to keep the covenant. The terms of the covenant [the observance of the 613 commandments of the Torah] remained unchanged, however, and the new covenant is merely a renewal of the Sinai covenant. Unlike the covenant at Sinai, which was broken, however, the new covenant will not be broken.

THE WORDS OF THE COVENANT

We will now examine how the Jewish commentaries understood the main verses of this passage:

Verse 30:

Why does it say: with the house of Israel and the house of Judah? Jeremiah lived at a time when the Northern Kingdom (Israel) had already been destroyed!

This indicates that the new covenant will be with both Israel and Judah. Since the ten tribes have still not been restored, the prophecy must be concerning a time that is still in the future.

The verse states that there will be *a new covenant but not a new Torah*. Since Israel failed to keep the old covenant, in the Messianic Age it will be necessary to form a new covenant which will not be broken.

Verse 32

What is the meaning of: and I will place my Torah in their midst and I will inscribe it upon their hearts?

This means that each Jew will have an automatic desire in their hearts to fulfill the commandments of the Torah. There will no longer be any desire to sin.

Question: An objection can be raised: one can only merit reward in response to activating one's free-will to perform a commandment.[98] If there is no desire to sin, there is no free-will!!

Answer:[99] Free-will is not an absolute. Each person has free-will parameters. Some levels are too hard and one is not punished for failing to achieve them. Others are too easy to accomplish and so one receives no reward for them. Within these two extremes lies each person's free-will parameters, e.g. a newly religious Jew will exert great self-discipline to resist non-kosher food, whereas an experienced scholar will have no trouble with this. At the other extreme, the scholar may be capable of disciplining

---

98   *See Covenant with Adam* for an explanation of the nature of free-will.

99   This answer is based on a principle found in *Michtav M'Eliahu* by Rabbi Eliahu Dessler, now translated into English under the title: *Strive For Truth*

himself to study Torah twenty hours a day, but the average person would find this quite impossible.

In the Messianic Age, the free-will parameters of every Jew will be raised to such a level of commitment that nobody will have any desire any more to transgress any of the commandments. It does not mean that there will be no free-will, but that free-will will then be used to choose ever better ways of observing the commandments.

Verse 33

Why will it no longer be necessary for anyone to teach his neighbour [to] know the Lord?

In the Messianic Age, there will be no confusion about G-d's existence. Those who had not known before will be deemed to have sinned in error and will therefore all be forgiven.

Verses 34-35

These verses indicate the eternity of the Jewish people. Just as the earth would cease to exist if there was no sun to illuminate the day so is it impossible for Israel to cease to exist. This is the ultimate comfort for Israel who, in the days of Jeremiah, stood on the threshold of an exile which continues down to the present day. The exile is to be a punishment, but it is only a punishment. It is the chastisement of a Loving Father who guarantees His People will be protected and will survive the exile. It also guarantees that they will never cease to be His People.

CONCLUSION

These words link the covenant with Jeremiah to all the previous covenants. When G-d created the world, He did so for a purpose. That purpose was conveyed to Mankind through the medium of a covenant. Mankind was given two opportunities to fulfill G-d's covenant: in the days from Adam to Noah (covenant with Adam); and in the days from Noah until Abraham (covenant with Noah). At this point, G-d selects Abraham, renews the covenant with him alone (covenant with Abraham) and promises him that He will enter into an eternal covenant with his descendants (covenant with Moses). From that point on, it will be their responsibility to be the example to the world (the Chosen People) of how G-d's purpose is to be fulfilled. The establishment of a monarchy (covenant with David) created the means to bring the world to its final goal and, even though Israel will have to first endure a long and painful exile, the goal originally set for Adam will ultimately be fulfilled (covenant with Jeremiah at the end of days.

THEMES FROM JEWISH SCRIPTURES:

G-D &

SUFFERING

JOB 1-14; 19; 38 & 42

WITH PARTICULAR REFERENCE TO:

- THE UNIQUE NATURE OF THE BOOK
- ITS PARTICULAR TEACHINGS ABOUT THE NATURE OF G-D
- ITS UNDERSTANDING OF THE NATURE OF THE SUFFERING OF THE JEWS

INTRODUCTION

The book of Job begins with a dialogue (sometimes also called the 'prologue') between G-d and the Satan. This dialogue concerns whether or not Job is to be considered a righteous person. In order to demonstrate Job's true worth, G-d agrees to Satan's suggestion that Job be afflicted with great suffering in order to test his loyalty.

The trials of suffering begin and Job suffers the death of all his children. He loses all his wealth and becomes impoverished as his various business concerns all fail. He is also afflicted physically by extremely painful and unpleasant diseases.

A large part of the book is taken up with four of Job's friends, known as the comforters, each in turn attempting to console Job and help him to come to terms with his suffering. Each one provides a different explanation for why Job is suffering but, one by one, all their explanations are rejected by Job who remains unconsoled.

At various points in the book, Job cries out to G-d to explain to him why he is suffering so and the major theme of the book is explaining how Job responds to and eventually copes with his suffering. At the end of the book, G-d appears to Job and explains everything and then restores everything to Job. Job eventually comes to terms with and accepts his suffering.

The main point of the book is to teach the principles of why people suffer and how to cope with suffering. The message of the book is that Job passes his test and G-d 'wins His argument' with the Satan. Every different kind of suffering is (apparently) alluded to at some point in the book. Those who are suffering are bidden to study the book of Job to find a parallel with their suffering and be comforted/consoled with the lesson the book teaches about how this particular type of suffering is to be borne.

WHY WAS THE BOOK WRITTEN?

The answer to this question is very much affected by the different opinions concerning when and by whom the book was written. It is the only book in the Tenach whose origin is shrouded in mystery. The Talmud[100] identifies numerous different opinions concerning its origin. We will examine four of them:

Opinion 1 - Job is Abraham. The Torah says very little about the early life of Abraham. He is introduced at the age of 70 (some say 75) as a person who has attained a level of greatness fitting for G-d to enter into a covenant with him. How did he attain this exalted level? The Torah does not say. According to this opinion, the Satan challenged G-d that Abraham was not worthy of G-d's covenant. The book of Job describes the tests given to Abraham/Job and his ability to pass these tests ultimately proves him worthy of G-d's covenant. According to this opinion the author is unknown, but it would have to be one of those identified by the Talmud as righteous people of that generation, such as Shem (the son of Noah) or Ever (the grandson of Shem).

Opinion 2 – Job is the Israelites in Egypt. According to this opinion, the book is a parable. There is no such person as Job; He is merely an allegorical representation of the Israelites during their slavery in Egypt. The sufferings of Job are a record of the sufferings during the slavery and the purpose of the book is to be a consolation and source of solace for the slaves.

Just as Job appeared to suffer without end, so did the Israelites. Their plight appeared to be utterly hopeless and thoroughly undeserved. Just as Job's suffering eventually ended and only then was he able to understand its purpose, so too will the Israelites' slavery eventually come to an end, following which they too will understand the purpose behind their suffering. According to this opinion, the author is Moses. Before he fled Egypt, he was divinely inspired to compose this work of consolation to give solace and support for his enslaved brothers.

Opinion 3 – Job is a righteous gentile. The Talmud[101], in describing the persecutions of Pharoah during the enslavement of the Israelites, identifies three principal advisors to the royal court: Bilaam, Job and Jethro. According to the Talmudic tale, it was the wicked Bilaam who advised Pharoah to throw all the Israelite boys into the sea. The idea was put to the rest of the royal court. Jethro and Job both realised that Pharoah was looking only for approval and not advice. Jethro could not be a party to such wickedness and fled to Midian. Job, however, neither approved nor disapproved, but remained silent.

It is not always clear which Talmudic narratives are to be understood literally and which ones are parables. If this story is to be taken literally, then the book of Job describes the suffering necessary for Job to atone for all the suffering that the Israelites endured in Egypt as a consequence of his silence. According to this opinion, the author is unknown and the purpose of the book is to teach the consequences of not resisting evil.

---

100   *TB:* Bava Basra 15a/15b
101   Sotah 11a; Sanhedrin 106a

Opinion 4 – Job is the Jewish people in exile. According to this opinion, the book of Job was written during the period of the Babylonian exile. It was one of the last Biblical books to be written. As with Opinion 2, the book is an allegory and there is no such person as Job. It was written to describe the suffering that the Jewish people would have to endure throughout their long and bitter exile. The purpose of the book (again as with Opinion 2) is to give comfort and solace for the persecutions of the exile. A Jew would find his suffering in the book of Job and be comforted with the belief that, when the exile finally ends (with the Messiah's coming) all suffering will cease and all previous suffering will finally be understood. The author is one of the last generation of prophets and it was written either during the Babylonian exile or the early Second Temple period.

CONCLUSION

Most Orthodox scholars accept the second or the fourth opinion. The Babylonian Talmud[102] even states quite categorically, in the opinion of Reish Lakish, that Job did not exist. Either way, in Jewish thought, the book of Job is not generally believed to be about the suffering of an individual. Orthodox scholars have always understood the main point of the book was to be the primary source of classical Jewish teachings on the purpose of suffering and of how to cope with tragedy.

In trying to understand this difficult book, we will particularly consider the commentaries of two of the greatest medieval scholars: Rabbi Solomon Yitzchaki (1040-1105) known as Rashi and Rabbi Moses ben Nachman (1194-1270) known as Ramban. Rashi's commentary on Tenach is considered the most important starting point for understanding the text. Ramban is considered the greatest of the Sephardi commentaries

---

102   Bava Bathra 15a

THE ROLE OF THE SATAN

There is a very big difference between the Jewish and Christian understandings of the role of the Satan (sometimes called the Devil).

In Christian teaching, Satan was an angel who 'fell from grace' and was punished by being cast out of Heaven to suffer for all eternity in the fires of eternal damnation. Ever since, the Satan has sought to ensnare people by enticing them to follow their desires and also 'fall from grace'. Those who succumb, of course, after death will be forced to suffer with him in Hell. The Satan, consequently, is wickedness personified, the master of cruelty and deception whose one and only desire is to bring suffering and destruction on all.

In the book of Job, therefore, according to Christian teaching, the Satan's role was to break Job's trust and belief in G-d by afflicting him with suffering. Really, the Satan's role was to justify himself. If even Job ultimately 'fell from grace' as well by turning away from G-d, this would prove that nobody could withstand suffering and he (Satan) should never have been cast out from Heaven in the first place. Of course, the Satan fails, Job remains steadfast in his righteousness and the Satan is exposed for the wicked being he really is.

In Jewish teaching, the role of the Satan is very different. He is believed to be a servant of G-d (an angel) who has been given the task of providing tests of faith for people. The purpose of setting these tests is to give people the opportunity pass them, thus actualising their potential to raise themselves to a higher level of Divine service and earning for themselves a greater reward in the next world.

The Talmud emphasises the positive aspect of the Satan's work in the maxim that: no person is set a test that they cannot pass. This does not mean, of course, that everybody passes every test; just that everybody has the potential/ability to pass the test. The Satan, therefore, is not evil. The tasks he sets, however, challenge people to fight against, resist and overcome evil. The Talmud further states that every time a person succumbs and gives in to his evil inclination, the Satan cries.

In the book of Job, therefore, the Satan's role is to test Job with suffering in order to find at what point he has an inclination to turn against G-d. It was only because of Job's greatness that such an enormous amount of suffering was necessary before Job's trust of G-d was challenged. At that point, Job is confronted with the need to resist his inclination and to stay loyal to G-d.

CHAPTER 1

THE DECISION

TO AFFLICT

JOB

1 *There was a man in the land of Uz, whose name was Job; and that man was whole-hearted and upright, and one that feared G-d, and shunned evil. 2 And there were born to him seven sons and three daughters. 3 His possessions also were seven thousand sheep, three thousand camels, five hundred yoke of oxen, five hundred she-asses and a very great household; so that this man was the greatest of all the children of the east. 4 And his sons used to go and hold a feast in the house of each one upon his day; and they would send and invite their three sisters to eat and to drink with them. 5 And it was when the days of their feasting were completed that Job sent and sanctified them and rose up early in the morning and offered burnt-offerings according to the number of them all; for Job said: 'It may be that my sons have sinned and blasphemed G-d in their hearts.' Thus did Job [act] continually. 6 Now it fell upon a day, that the sons [angels] of G-d came to present themselves before Him and Satan came also among them. 7 And G-d said to Satan: 'From where have you come?' and Satan answered G-d and said: 'From going to and fro in the earth and from walking up and down in it.' 8 And G-d said to Satan: 'Have you considered My servant Job, that there is none like him in the earth, a whole-hearted and an upright man, that fears G-d, and shuns evil?' 9 Then Satan answered G-d and said: 'Does Job really fear G-d? 10 Have You not made a hedge about him and his house and all that he has on every side? You have blessed the work of his hands and his possessions are increased in the land. 11 But put forth Your hand now, and touch all that he has; surely he will blaspheme You to Your face.' 12 And G-d said to Satan: 'Behold, all that he has is in your power; only upon himself do not put forth your hand.' So Satan went out from the presence of G-d. 13 And it fell on a day when his sons and daughters were eating and drinking wine in their eldest brother's house. 14 There came a messenger to Job, and said: 'The oxen were ploughing and the donkeys feeding beside them. 15 And the Sabeans made a raid and took them away; they have slain [all] the servants with the edge of the sword; I alone have escaped to tell you.' 16 While he was yet speaking there came also another and said: 'A fire of G-d has fallen from heaven and has burned up the sheep and the servants, and consumed them; I alone have escaped to tell you.' 17 While he was yet speaking there came also another and said: 'The Chaldeans set themselves in three bands and fell upon the camels; they have taken them away and slain the servants with the edge of the sword; I alone have escaped to tell you.' 18 While he was yet speaking there came also another and said: 'Your sons and your daughters were eating and drinking wine in their eldest brother's house. 19 And behold there came a great wind from across the wilderness and smote the four corners of the house and it fell upon the young people and they are dead; I alone escaped to tell you.' 20 Then Job arose and tore his cloak and shaved his head and fell down upon the ground and prostrated himself. 21 And he said: Naked I came out of my mother's womb, and naked shall I return; G-d gave and G-d has taken away, may the name of G-d be blessed. 22 In all this, Job did not sin or ascribe impropriety to G-d.*

The decision

We are introduced to Job as an upright and honest man who lived in the land of Utz. No effort is made to identify when Job lived and we have no clue as to the location of Utz. This strengthens the point of view that Job is not a historical figure and the book should be viewed as a parable.[103]

The listing of Job's children and great wealth indicate how blessed he was. The number ten (his children) naturally symbolises completion and he was the wealthiest man in the whole region. His children would organise rounds of feasts, taking turns to be host and to invite the others. This indicates a warm and close family who care for each other. At the end of each cycle of feasts, Job would offer atonement sacrifices on behalf of each of his children, just in case they unwittingly sinned during their feasts. This further indicates that Job was a responsible father, continuing to do for his children even after they had grown up.

One day the angels appeared before G-d and Satan was with them. G-d asked Satan where he was coming from and he replied that he had been searching the earth. The Rabbis understand this to mean he had been searching the hearts of people with tests of their belief in G-d.

G-d asked Satan if he had taken note of Job, a man the likes of whom could not be found in all the earth in fear of G-d and avoidance of sin. Satan answers that Job has no reason to fear G-d since G-d constantly protects him from harm and blesses all his endeavours. If G-d would turn against him, then see if Job will not curse Him, even to His face.

Satan's point is that Job's righteousness has not been sufficiently tested. He is not arguing with G-d, merely saying that what G-d is saying has not yet been proven to be true. Only if he were afflicted with a degree of suffering that would make a lesser man curse G-d to His face could it then be shown that Job was truly righteous if he did not do the same.

G-d answers Satan and instructs him to afflict Job accordingly. Although this dialogue is written in the form of a disagreement between G-d and Satan, that is not what is really happening. If G-d says something it must be true. Nobody can prove G-d wrong. What Satan is saying is that, whilst G-d may know the true level of Job, it has not been shown to Job himself. Only by putting him to the test can he actually rise to the level that G-d knows he can reach. G-d would not permit Satan to afflict Job with suffering unless Job could withstand the test.

---

103   Rambam: Guide for the Perplexed III:22

The afflictions begin

One day, whilst his children were enjoying one of their feasts, a messenger came to tell Job that whilst the oxen were ploughing and the she-donkeys were grazing, a band of Sabeans attacked them and captured them all, killing all the men except for this one messenger who managed to escape. These are the animals that work to produce the goods from which the wealth is made.

Whilst he was still speaking, another one of Job's men entered to report that a freak fire had consumed all the flocks and killed all the shepherds that were with them, except for this one messenger who managed to escape. The flocks are primarily raised for their food.

Whilst he was still speaking, another one of Job's men entered to report that the Chaldeans had attacked and captured all the camels. They had killed all the men except for this one messenger who managed to escape. The camels transport Job's goods to market for him to sell there.

Whilst he was still speaking, another one of Job's men entered to report that he had come from the feast of Job's children. Whilst they were feasting, a desert wind (hurricane?) engulfed the house, causing it to collapse upon the people inside, killing them all except for this one messenger who managed to escape. Finally, the children were the ones for whom all the wealth was created.

Job responds

Job stood up and tore his cloak and the hair on his head. He prostrated himself on the ground and said:

> Naked did I emerge from my mother's womb and naked will I return. G-d has given and G-d has taken away. May the Name of G-d be blessed.

Job did not speak out against G-d.

Job's response is an exceptional example of righteousness and humility. The number of different disasters that all happened at the same time is proof positive for Job that this is an affliction from G-d. He acknowledges that all his great wealth was merely a gift of G-d and not something that he had necessarily earned at all. As such, he could have no complaint if it was taken away. Similarly, children are put in this world for their own purpose and parents are merely stewards of G-d, taking care of them on His behalf. If He chooses to 'take them home' there is nothing for a parent to complain about.

This initial response of Job to his suffering has become the quintessential Jewish answer to suffering. These verses are now recited in the Orthodox funeral service as an expression of faith in the justice of G-d's rule.

CHAPTER 2

THE

AFFLICTIONS

INTENSIFY

1. And it was upon a day, that the sons [angels] of G-d came to present themselves before G-d and Satan came also among them to present himself before G-d. 2. And G-d said to Satan: 'From where have you come?' And Satan answered G-d and said: 'From going to and fro in the earth, and from walking up and down in it.' 3. And G-d said to Satan: 'Have you considered my servant Job, that there is none like him in the earth, a whole-hearted and an upright man, one that fears G-d and shuns evil and still holds fast his integrity, although you moved Me against him, to destroy him without cause?' 4. And Satan answered G-d and said: 'Limb for limb, all that a man has will he give up for his life. 5. But stretch out Your hand now, and strike his bone and his flesh, surely he will blaspheme You to Your face.' 6. And G-d said unto Satan: 'Behold, he is in your hand; only spare his life.' 7. So Satan went out from G-d's presence and afflicted Job with sore boils from the sole of his foot to the crown of his head. 8. And he took a shard to scrape himself and he sat among the ashes. 9. Then said his wife to him: 'Do you still maintain your integrity? - blaspheme G-d and die.' 10. But he said to her: 'You speak as one of the impious women speaks; shall we accept good at the hand of G-d and not accept evil?'- in all this Job did not sin with his lips.

11. Now when Job's three friends heard of all these calamities that had befallen him, they came every one from his own place - Eliphaz the Temanite, and Bildad the Shuhite, and Tzophar the Naamathite - and met together to come to mourn with him and to comfort him. 12. And when they lifted up their eyes from afar they recognised him not; they raised their voice, and wept; and each one tore his garment and threw dust into the air over their heads. 13. They sat with him on the ground for seven days and for seven nights, and none spoke a word to him for they saw that his grief was very great. 14. Afterwards Job began to speak and cursed the day of his birth.

The Satan's Request

Once again, the angels appeared before G-d and the Satan was with them. G-d again asked the Satan where he was coming from and again he replied that he had been searching the earth. Again, G-d asked the Satan if he had taken note of Job, a man the likes of whom could not be found in all the earth in fear of G-d and avoidance of sin.

The point of the repetition is to emphasise that, despite all that had happened since the last time the heavenly hosts had convened, nothing had changed in Job's trust and faith in G-d. In other words, he had passed his test.

G-d reproaches the Satan that: *...you incited Me to devour him for no good reason.* The implication is that there had been no need to inflict the suffering upon him. This does not mean that Job suffered for nothing. Rather, this means that, even after all this suffering, Job had not yet been challenged sufficiently to be tempted to turn away from G-d. In other words, the test had not been hard enough!

The Satan now requests that he be given permission to afflict Job with physical pain as this is the most intense and difficult of all pains to bear. G-d gives permission to the Satan to afflict Job providing he spares his life. The Satan departs and strikes Job with severe boils from the tips of his feet to the top of his head.

Job responds

Job took a shard to scratch himself and sat in ashes. His wife bade him to curse G-d and die, but he reproved her for such a suggestion. He answered: *Will we accept the good from G-d and not the bad?*

The meaning of this is that, when good things happen to us we do not investigate to see whether or not we deserve them. Even if we do investigate, we invariably find that in truth we do not deserve them, yet we still accept G-d's beneficence. If we accept the good decrees that we do not deserve, then we must accept the bad decrees that we do not deserve as well.

This is a very significant change. In Chapter 1, Job accepted that his suffering was just. In Chapter 2, he does not acknowledge that it was just, only that it was something that he must accept. It says: *...Job did not sin with his lips.* This means that he did not say out loud any complaint, but deep down he felt it was unjust.

It is also interesting to note the first reference to Job's wife. We are indirectly informed of her righteousness as well. She also suffered the loss of wealth and the death of all her children but did not complain. Only now, when she is not suffering herself, does she complain! A good wife feels the pain of her husband's suffering more than her own suffering.

Job's comforters arrive

Job had three companions, living in different parts of the country. Their names were Eliphaz the Teimanite, Bildad the Shuhite and Tzofar the Na'amatite. When they heard of Job's misfortune, they came to visit him. They first met and decided that together they would come and offer him comfort. When they saw him from afar, however, they could not recognise him. They wept and tore their cloaks; they put dust on their heads and sat with him on the floor for seven days and nights. Nobody said anything for they saw that his suffering was very great.

A number of Jewish mourning laws are indicated here:

1] It is a mitzvah to visit a mourner in order to comfort him;

2] It is customary to perform *keriyah* [the tearing of an outer garments]
   when hearing of or being present at the death of a relative or a great
   person;

3] Intense mourning, known as *shivah*, lasts for seven days;

4] A mourner sits on the floor or on a low stool for those seven days;

5] One does not speak to a mourner but merely responds when addressed;

The greatness of the comforters in indicated here. The Rabbis ask: did Job only have three companions? They were the only ones who overcame their own uncomfortableness to be able to visit Job and try to comfort him.

CHAPTER 3

JOB

QUESTIONS

HIS

SUFFERING

This is a very difficult chapter to decipher and there are a number of different version both of the translation and the structure of the verses (some divide it into 25 and others into 26 verses). For the first time, Job speaks out against his suffering.

In the first half of this chapter, Job curses the day on which he was born. This is understood as a reference to astrology. The astrological forces exert an influence on life on this planet. Normally, G-d will 'amend' the influence of the astrological forces according to a person's merit. Job is bemoaning the fact that the forces in operation on the day that he was born have not been affected by G-d's influence. Alternatively, had this day been omitted from the calendar altogether, Job would never have been born! This would have been better than the suffering he now has to endure. Rashi and Ramban explain this point differently:

Rashi understands the book of Job to be a compendium of the varieties of different forms of suffering that a human being can experience. Job is overcome with anguish at his misfortune. Why is G-d allowing 'nature' to treat him so harshly? He has questions but no answers. **He is not angry with G-d but with his own inability to see any good in his suffering**.

Ramban, on the other hand, understands Job to be reaching a theological conclusion. G-d created the astrological forces and then left the world to 'nature'. **Job is not suffering because G-d is 'afflicting' him but because G-d seems to not be 'involved' in his existence**.

In the second half of the chapter, Job questions whether life itself has value. Job is only questioning the value of life in this world, not the world to come. In this world, all must eventually die, so once one is afflicted with suffering, what is the value to prolonging life?

Both would agree that, whereas in Chapter 1 Job accepted the bad with the good, i.e. acknowledged the justice of G-d's actions, in Chapter 3 he expresses a weary resignation to his fate. Eventually, he even questions whether life is worth living if this is his fate.

It is reasonable to assume that Job's questions of this chapter must coincide with the seven days of silence during which the comforters sat with Job. The following chapters deal with their efforts to comfort Job and can be understood as a response to these questions. Since Rashi and Ramban understand Job's questions differently, they also understand the comforters' responses differently, as we shall see.

THE

THREE

COMFORTERS

One of the principal features of the first half of the book of Job is the attempts made by Job's three friends to comfort/console him in his suffering. Each one in turn approaches Job and, in response to Job's anguish, presents a suggested explanation for why Job is suffering. Each one in turn has his explanation rejected by Job.

If the book of Job is understood as a parable, then **the comforters are not real people**. Rather, the author wishes to present **different rationales for why people suffer**. Instead of explaining each perspective in technical detail, which would be a very complex thing to do and would be comprehensible only to the greatest scholars, instead he chooses to tell a story. Each of the comforters 'acts' the perspective of a different rationale so that, as the story unfolds, all explanations of suffering are inserted. In this way, **the concept of suffering is presented in a way that is accessible to all.**

Each comforter in turn, consequently, presents a perfectly valid explanation for why some people suffer. Each comforter is correct, up to a point. **When all the comforters' are put together, we then have a comprehensive explanation of why** most **people suffer.** Most individual Jews, therefore, will be able to identify a connection between their own personal suffering and something said by one of the comforters.

There will remain, however, a small number of people who fail to find any personal connection or consolation from any of the statements of the comforters. These people must identify with Job, the one who does not understand why he is suffering. G-d's answer to Job at the end of the book provides the solace for these people.

CHAPTER 4-5

ELIPHAZ

THE

FIRST

COMFORTER

In Chapter Three, Job has expressed his dismay at his present condition. Eliphaz responds to Job's statement:

According to Rashi: Eliphaz implores Job to look inwards. Instead of complaining at his inability to understand his fate, Job should concentrate on improving his inner self and thereby coming closer to G-d.

According to Ramban: Eliphaz seeks to challenge Job's conclusion that he is the victim of astrological forces, an unfortunate 'coincidence of circumstances'. He emphasises that Job's suffering is a direct visitation of G-d, even if he does not understand why it is happening.

Eliphaz begins from the perspective that **if Job is suffering that in itself indicates he must be a sinner.** He must have done wrong in order to bring suffering upon himself. He opens with what is almost a rebuke. Is Job wearied (4:1) by his test? The Rabbis understand from this that **G-d would not give anybody suffering too difficult to bear.** In the past, Job has strengthened others in their suffering, so why is he now unable to cope when suffering comes to him? Eliphaz asks:

> Consider if you will: what innocent man has ever perished?... those who plough iniquity and sow trouble harvest [just] that. By G-d's blast they perish and by the heat of His anger they are consumed.[104]

Eliphaz takes the principle of Ethical Monotheism to its logical conclusion.

According to Rashi, all suffering should lead one to introspection and self-improvement.

According to Ramban, one should never mistakenly see one's misfortune as 'coincidence'.

Either way, Eliphaz makes the point that **there is an ethical G-d who deals with every human being in fairness.**

G-d will not bring suffering upon someone if they do not deserve it. It is impossible to conclude, therefore, that one who is suffering can be anything but a sinner. **His advice to Job is to accept his suffering as a punishment for his sins and to repent.** He should take comfort in the fact that, since he is still alive, he has not been judged to be completely evil. He should realise that his punishment could have been worse and he should not complain about his portion.

---

104   Job 4:7-9

Conclusion

Eliphaz is the first comforter because:

According to Rashi, when a person is suffering, the first question to be asked of oneself is whether that suffering might be the atonement for one's sins.

According to Ramban, it is because the instinctive first reaction to suffering is to see it as 'bad luck' rather than a consequence of one's actions.

If one is able to respond honestly that this is not the case, then one can move on to consider the next rationale for why people suffer. According to Rabbinic tradition, most people will find their answer in Eliphaz's explanation.

JOB

RESPONDS

TO

ELIPHAZ

In these two chapters Job forcefully rejects the explanation of Eliphaz.

According to Rashi:

Eliphaz's call to look inwards is pointless for all his experience indicates that **G-d wishes to do him harm.** All his past accomplishments have been destroyed and the future lies before him as an utterly futile existence.

According to Ramban:

Eliphaz's actual message has been accepted, but it creates a worse scenario than before! Job acknowledges that he is not the luckless victim of coincidence, but that **he has been singled out by G-d for exceptional suffering.** Instead of his previous picture (in Chapter Three) in which he saw G-d as being uninvolved, Eliphaz presents him with a picture of G-d being totally uncaring of his plight. **G-d, as it were, is 'too busy' to involve Himself in the needs of one small and insignificant person such as Job.**

At the beginning of Chapter 6, Job answers Eliphaz that he has inspected his deeds and whilst he does not believe himself to be free from sin, he can honestly and dispassionately conclude that nothing he has done in his lifetime could possibly justify the suffering that he is enduring now. He also rejects Eliphaz's conclusion that death would be a worse punishment than he is presently suffering. He says:

> The terrors of G-d have been rained upon me... If only my request were granted ... and G-d would agree to crush me [completely]; let Him release His hand and finish me off. This would still be a consolation for me...[105]

G-d would do him a favour by ending his life, according to Rashi, because nothing of value awaits him in the future. According to Ramban, the fact that He does not end his life is evidence of His lack of consideration for Job's needs. **Job admonishes Eliphaz for not recognising the extent of his suffering in relation to the person he is.** He also criticises his failure to give him any constructive advice as to how to cope with his situation.

> Teach me and I will be silent; help me understand what error I have made... but what point is there in the arguments which you have given? [Are] words alone an argument?... [Y]ou would dig a pit for your companion.[106]

---

105   Job 6:4-10
106   Job 6:24-27

In Chapter 7, Job makes a moving declaration of the insignificance of human life. In the first half of the chapter, he focuses on its shortness; in the second half, on its irrelevance. In the 'wider picture', he concludes, G-d surely has no reason to even consider the needs of one solitary individual.

Eliphaz, of course, has already rejected Job's capacity to even judge the situation. He must accept G-d's judgement of him as a sinner.

CONCLUSION

Eliphaz is rejected for having made Job's situation worse.

According to Rashi, Job rejects Eliphaz's judgement of him as a sinner.

According to Ramban, Eliphaz's picture of an uncaring G-d is worse than Job's original picture of a G-d uninvolved in the world.

According to both, Eliphaz has failed to identify with Job as a person. The wider message of Job's speech is that there are times when one feels abandoned or ignored by G-d. They must seek a different route if they are to cope with their suffering.

CHAPTER 8

BILDAD

THE
SECOND
COMFORTER

Bildad applies the concept of retribution even more strongly than Eliphaz.

According to Rashi: Bildad also suggests that Job's suffering may be the wages of sin (v. 3). Job must examine his past to see if there is anything there for which he is entitled to suffer. Even if there is not, the present suffering indicates that Job's future will surely be bright for all his iniquity will have been atoned for. Whereas Eliphaz suggests Job look inside himself to identify his failings as a person, **Bildad suggests he look back to identify the errors of his past.**

According to Ramban:

Bildad dismisses the death of Job's children almost as an irrelevance! They died for their own sins which are possibly unknown (and unknowable) to Job. Bildad accepts that Job's personal suffering is not for the purpose of bringing him closer to G-d. **Rather it is a form of cleansing him,** a purification process that is eradicating all trace of sin from him.

The death of Job's children

Bildad focuses first upon the death of Job's family and suggests that it was their punishment and not Job's punishment. **If they died, then it was because of their own sins** and nothing to do with Job. He advises:

> *Would G-d pervert judgement; would the Almighty pervert justice?*
> *When your children sinned against Him, He used their own transgre*
> *ssion to take them away...*[107]

In essence, Bildad is focusing on the perfection of G-d and the boundaries of Man's free-will. Nobody can die unless G-d decrees it. G-d would not decree it if it was not just. **Since Job is still alive, however, his suffering is to be seen as relatively minor, it was his children who were really being punished.**

According to Bildad, there is a strict limitation to free-will. Man only has the freedom to want to do something. Whether or not the intention actually produces the desired action is up to G-d. His perspective on suffering is very stark, but relevant in some cases. There are times when people die unexpectedly and it is a punishment for their sins. However unpleasant a thought this may be for the mourner, nevertheless it is something that sometimes happens.

According to both Rashi and Ramban, the death of others is unfathomable to us. According to Rashi, it is something we accept without questioning. According to Ramban, it is not even considered a part of our suffering.

---

107   Job 8:3-4

The metaphor of the reed

Bildad compares the wicked to the reed which, when uprooted from its source of water, is the first of the plants to wither and die. So is it with man, when he uproots himself from the ways of G-d he too withers and dies spiritually. G-d's ways are compared to water for both are the principal source of sustenance, the one spiritual the other physical.

According to Rashi, this is a warning to Job to remain the righteous person he is despite his present suffering.

According to Ramban, it is an ultimatum: accept your suffering or be banished to oblivion.

Bildad's conclusion of hope

By the end of the chapter, however, it is clear that Bildad's words are intended as a comfort to Job, who identifies only with his own suffering. Similarly, it is customary for mourners to blame themselves for the death of a loved one (if only I had done this/ said that/been there for him or her). Bildad is telling Job that he must not blame himself for the death of his family. They died for their own sins. His own personal suffering, however, is merely temporary and all he needs to do is to perfect his service of G-d and he will have even more than he had before, as he says:

> Your beginning will seem small but your end will prosper greatly...[108]

According to Rashi, this means that, after he has been purified, he will reap the rewards of his purity. According to Ramban, by completing his repentance, he will be worthy of a better future. This optimistic message is further consolidated at the end of the chapter:

> ... G-d will not reject the innocent... He will yet fill your mouth with laughter and your lips with joyous shouting... (but) the tent of the wicked shall cease to be.[109]

---

108   Job 8:7
109   Job 8:20-22

CHAPTER 9-10

JOB

RESPONDS

TO

BILDAD

According to Rashi: Job utterly rejects Bildad's explanation of his suffering. He sees himself as the victim of unmerited cruelty. There is no path of correction open to him, or even a hearing from G-d. He regrets that he was even born if it was to suffer so, but at the end of the speech implores G-d to end his suffering that he may enjoy what remains of his life in tranquillity.

According to Ramban: Job responds that it appears that there is no difference between the treatment of the wicked and the righteous. All appear to suffer and die. He is bewildered by his treatment for which there is no rational solution. Does G-d need to demonstrate His strength or give meaningless tests?

Job's apparent blasphemy

Even though Job's answer to Bildad contains many similarities to the one he gave to Eliphaz, nevertheless it is far more strident. He acknowledges the impossibility of challenging G-d for: how can a mortal win his case against G-d?[110] He poetically describes G-d's overwhelming strength and power. Yet he will not acknowledge that he is a sinner for he knows deep in his heart that this is not true. He complains that:

> *I am faultless [but] know no rest... There is one [fate for all]... He destroys both the faultless and the wicked*[111]

Job elaborates on this cry in the rest of Chapter 9. There seems to be no point to repentance or to righteousness for all seem to suffer the same fate. According to Rashi, Job is bemoaning the injustice of his own circumstances. According to Ramban, Job's cry is a reference to those who look at the world and see righteous people suffering whilst wicked people prosper. Where is the reward for righteousness? Who can see it?

Job challenges G-d

In Chapter 10, Job addresses G-d with the same cry that he gave in response to Bildad. He pleads with G-d to: let me know of what You are accusing me.[112] He implores G-d to acknowledge his innocence whilst at the same time submitting humbly to His authority:

> *You know I will do no evil... none can save [me] from Your hand.*[113]

---

110   Job 9:2
111   Job 9:21
112   Job 10:2
113   Job 10:7

Both Rashi and Ramban understand Job to be expressing his refusal to succumb to the temptation of blasphemy, even if all his suffering is merely to goad him into just such a response.

Job continues to protest throughout the rest of this chapter that, if this is his lot, then what purpose has been served in giving him life? Only, it is not just his life that has no purpose but all life in G-d's world, if this is its reward.

Rashi explains Job's 'complaint' to be a rejection not of his suffering, but of his not being given an explanation for why he is suffering.

Ramban, however, does see Job rejecting his suffering. If this is his lot, then his life has no meaning and he cannot see any purpose on its being continued. If a person has sinned and suffering is intended to bring him to repentance, then it is essential that the sinner understands the link between his sin and the suffering. Otherwise, what purpose does the suffering serve?
Alternatively, if a person has sinned and the suffering is his punishment, then it is essential that the sinner understands what sin he is punished for to avoid future repetition. In that case, the suffering will surely continue.

Finally, if a person has not sinned at all, then why is he suffering? If there is another reason for his suffering, then how can the suffering achieve its purpose if the one suffering does not understand why he is suffering?

At the end of the chapter, Job considers his own death for: *Are my days not few and coming to an end?*[114] and begs for a brief respite before *the gloom and the shadow of death*[115] overtake him.

---

114   Job 10:20
115   Job 10:22

CHAPTER 11

TZOPHAR

THE

THIRD

COMFORTER

Whereas both Eliphaz and Bildad tried to minimise Job's culpability, Tzophar views him in a completely different light. He suggests that even though Job appears to be an extremely righteous person, nevertheless, the very fact that he is going through such suffering clearly indicates that **Job must be much more of a sinner than anybody realises.** Rashi and Ramban differ only on the source of Tzophar's points, not on its intrinsic meaning.

According to Rashi: Tzophar is supplying an alternative explanation for Job's suffering. Job must have an 'evil' side of him of which the world knows nothing at all. If Job really could recognise G-d, he would then realise that it would be totally impossible for Him to visit suffering on any other than one whose sins deserved it.

According to Ramban: Tzophar is focusing on the near-blasphemous answers of Job to Bildad's words. It is not for Job to reject his suffering but (as Rashi also says) to recognise G-d and acknowledge his own culpability. Job's answer to Bildad was a denial of the justice of G-d and Tzophar responds that **Job should not be stubbornly protesting his own righteousness.**

G-d's intrinsic attribute of mercy

Tzophar presents the most extreme version of retribution so far. He differs from what has gone before by emphasising the principle that G-d, who is known to be merciful to all, will always give people less punishment than they really deserve.

> *You say [to G-d]: My way is pure [and] I am innocent before You...*
> *if G-d would speak... He would tell you... that by right [you deserve]*
> *twice as much...*[116]

It is a fundamental principle of Judaism, applied in many places (particularly in reference to the High Holy Day period), that G-d tempers His justice with mercy. Every human being, consequently, had they been judged strictly according to the dictates of justice, would receive far more suffering than they actually do. **Job, therefore, by the same calculation, must also have received less suffering than his conduct deserved.**

What Tzophar is really saying is that **we do not really know how righteous any other person actually is.** We know what we see, but what about the secret actions of a person that take place when nobody is present? What about the innermost desires and forbidden thoughts that people may indulge in? Only G-d appreciates the true value of a person.

---

116   Job 11:4-6

Man's inability to understand G-d's ways

Tzophar goes on to describe the absolute impossibility of comprehending G-d's plans.

Can you attain a complete knowledge of G-d?... what can you know?...
if he were to pass by who could turn Him back?[117]

According to Rashi, this means that Job is wrong to consider himself undeserving of punishment for how can he be sure he has not fallen short of G-d's expectations for him.

According to Ramban, Tzophar is emphasising the fact that G-d is fully aware of everything that is happening to Job and therefore it must be an appropriate form of suffering for him to endure.

Job must acknowledge the justice of his treatment

Tzophar calls upon Job to accept the justice of his afflictions by focusing his attention on his own shortcomings:

If you would correct your heart and spread forth your hands [in
prayer] towards Him... then you will be free of imperfection...[118]

This can be understood both literally and figuratively. Job would be 'free' of his physical sufferings for his repentance would cause G-d to heal him. Also, he would be free from the spiritual blemish of sin for he would have accepted the justice of his suffering and this would have caused his sin to be eradicated.

CONCLUSION

Whereas Eliphaz minimised Job's failings and Bildad bade Job focus on the brightness of his future, Tzophar forcefully demands that Job face his own unworthiness and accept it.

According to Rashi, Tzophar points to the solution to coping with suffering. It is having the humility to accept it.

According to Ramban, Tzophar demands that, even though we live in a world where wicked people prosper, righteous people must accept the justice of their suffering.

---

117   Job 11:7-10
118   Job 11:13-15

CHAPTER 12-14

JOB

RESPONDS

TO

TZOPHAR

Both Rashi and Ramban find difficulty in finding anything different in what Job says now to what he has already said in answer to Eliphaz and Bildad. Possibly, it is here that Job brings all the points from the first series of speeches together and his answer is for all of the comforters and not just for Tzophar.

According to Rashi: Job is torn between acknowledging the unknowable nature of G-d's ways and bemoaning the misery and wretchedness of his own situation. **He wants to accept G-d's treatment of him but he cannot.** It would be the height of hypocrisy for him to do anything but assert his rejection of his treatment.

According to Ramban: Job continues to be troubled by the tranquillity enjoyed by the wicked in comparison to his own situation. **Is G-d so exalted high above us that He is indifferent to human suffering,** so long as the Divine plan is achieved? Or is G-d truly the author of Job's suffering, in which case what is the point of it all?

In Chapter 12, Job's answer to Tzophar is very scathing. He rejects his philosophy of retribution and assumption of Job's inferiority. In verse 3, Job retorts: I am no less than you. If Tzophar be listened to then he would be a laughing-stock (v.4) and completely degraded in the eyes of all.

According to Rashi, this is Job rejecting the injustice of his treatment.

According to Ramban (who translates the words slightly differently) it is a restatement of **the apparent indifference of G-d to his suffering.**

At the same time, paradoxically, **Job does not deny G-d's providence.** Referring to the natural order of the world in verse 9, he asks rhetorically: Who would not know from all these [phenomena] that this is G-d's handiwork? He claims that G-d is just but **His justice is not fathomable** to humans who: grope in the dark without illumination... (v.25)

According to Rashi, Job knows G-d is just to all but His justice is unfathomable to man.

According to Ramban, G-d's justice is revealed in the accomplishment of the Divine plan, but not in the lives of individual human beings.

In this chapter, the central feature of Job's response to suffering is highlighted vividly. He harshly rebukes his comforters for assuming his wickedness and thus failing to comfort him at all. At the same time, however, Job has not lost his faith in G-d. But he has lost his ability to understand why G-d is acting towards him as He is. He does not even request that his suffering stop, only that he be given the ability to comprehend what is happening to him.

In Chapter 13, Job emphasises that his knowledge and understanding of his situation as at least equal to that of the comforters. The chapter opens with his declaration:

> *Indeed my eye has seen it all; my ear has heard and understood it.*
> *I also know what you know; I am no less than you.*[119]

He does not wish to engage with them but with G-d. He utterly rejects the notion that his suffering has anything to do with punishment and accuses the comforters of having failed in their task of comforting him. Rashi points out that this teaches a lesson in the law of comforting a mourner. Even though the comforters genuinely believed that what they were saying would be a comfort to Job, nevertheless they antagonised and upset him. Similarly, when visiting a mourner once must take extra care not to say anything that could be misunderstood or taken the wrong way.

Job accuses the comforters of trying to ingratiate themselves with G-d by suggesting that His actions were just when they did not really understand them themselves. This is a hint to those who are quick to identify fault in others and have excellent 'advice' for how others can lead more righteous lives. They would do better to direct their advice at themselves!

Job realises that he might jeopardise his own situation by complaining to G-d, but he is determined to be nothing less than totally honest, no matter what the cost. His faith remains that, by being brutally honest, G-d will not forsake him:

> *Though He might kill me I will place my hope in Him... let me defend*
> *my ways before Him. He is also my salvation [but] if I am now silent*
> *I will perish.*[120]

Rashi understands Job here as being defiant in his humility. Acknowledging G-d, but confessing his inability to accept the apparent injustice of his suffering.

Ramban, on the other hand, understands Job to be seeking an answer so that he can benefit from his suffering. His complaint is at the pointlessness of his present situation.

Modern psychology agrees with the idea expressed here. Someone who feels a genuine need to complain or protest but, out of fear of rejection or punishment, does not say anything, will only build up a wall of resentment and stifled anger. It is far healthier to express complaints than to bottle them up.

---

119   Job 13:1-2
120   Job 13:15-19

In verse 21, Job asks G-d to Remove Your hand from me and, in verse 23, to … *inform me of my iniquity and sin.* He begs for a respite from a punishment that is so hard to bear and at the same time asks G-d to explain the relationship between his suffering and his conduct. His humility before G-d is poetically expressed, as he compares himself, in verse 25, to a driven leaf and a piece of dry straw in the hands of the All-powerful Master of the Universe.

In Chapter 14, Job focuses first on the shortness of a human life:

> *Like a flower he blossoms and then withers; like a shadow he flees and is gone.*[121]

Is there any point in man's suffering being prolonged? One who is no longer able to enjoy the fullness of life would prefer the release of death. Modern scholars have speculated that, possibly, the argument for euthanasia is hinted at in these verses.

> *…You have fixed his days, the number of his months is with You; You have fixed his boundaries and he cannot pass. Leave him be, that he may rest…*[122]

Whilst Jewish law unequivocally opposes euthanasia, nevertheless it recognises that the desire of the old or infirm to die can be very real. Job poetically expresses the misery of the terminally ill patient for whom all hope of a meaningful future existence has ended. Jewish law does not permit suicide or assisted suicide, but it recognises the desire for such an ending exists. And just as Job is portrayed as one with whom we identify and empathise, so should the terminal sufferer be treated with compassion and concern.

From verse 7 until the end of the chapter (v.22) Job bemoans the frailty and helplessness of the human condition. Unlike a tree which, if cut down can grow again, when a human being dies he is gone forever. Just like the mountain, the rock or stones that are eroded and carried away by the constant flow of the water, so is a human being gone forever when he dies.

According to Rashi, Job is now despairing of any end to his suffering.

Ramban, however, interpret these verses more optimistically. Job is referring only to the death of the physical body, which has no more permanence than a rock or a stone that is washed away by the tide and is gone. He actually welcomes death, which will free him from the suffering of his body and release his soul to enjoy the rewards of the next world.

---

121   Job 14:2
122   Job 14:5-6

CONCLUSION

If we understand the book of Job as a parable, then the dialogue between Job and the comforters begins in Chapter 2 when Job cries out against his suffering. Eliphaz, the first comforter seeks to answer Job's cry. His answer will have relevance for many who suffer, but Job's response reflects those for whom this is not the answer. The process is repeated by Bildad and again by Tzophar.

> The essential sameness of the ideas put forward by the [comforters] makes the... differences... of Job's [responses] significant... [H]is response to Eliphaz consists entirely of a bemoaning of his fate; that to Bildad is a heart-rending plea for understanding...; that which follows Tzophar [is] a rebuttal of [all] three...[123]

The point of these dialogues would not be to explain Job's suffering as such. Rather, it would be to show that, even after all their solutions have been presented, there will still be those for whom, like Job, there are no answers just misery and anguish and an inability to understand.

Possibly, the comforters provide the rationale for understanding the 'normal' suffering that people experience. Job represents the extreme, the victim of a pogrom or a crusade, in which entire villages were destroyed and their populations brutalised. How does the survivor of such an ordeal find 'answers' for their suffering? Does G-d see? Does G-d care? Can anyone explain it for them? We can only accept, in silence, that we do not understand. That is Job's answer to the advice of the comforters at the end of Chapter 14.

---

[123]   Rabbi Moshe Eisemann: Artscroll Job p. 163

CHAPTER 15-18

[not in the syllabus]

In Chapter 15, Eliphaz returns to reprove Job for the answers he has given to the first series of speeches. Job has refused to accept the justice of his suffering. This, in itself, says Eliphaz, demonstrates its justice! Job, as it were, is condemned by his own words.

In Chapters 16-17, Job answers Eliphaz's second speech. He again focuses on his suffering being undeserved and that it suggests G-d is not concerned with the specific fate of individuals. Whilst there are no new points made by Job in these chapters, the intensity of his description of the injustice is much stronger.

In Chapter 18, Bildad returns to continue where Eliphaz left off. He emphasises the awesome emptiness that is the ultimate fate that awaits the wicked, to which Job will be subjected unless he acknowledges the justice of his suffering. Earlier, Bildad had focused on the death of Job's children. Job naturally saw his children as his future, which now exists no more. In this speech, Bildad focuses on the bereaved father who must accept his fate and move on.

CHAPTER 19

JOB RESPONDS TO BILDAD'S SECOND SPEECH

In this response, Job pleads for mercy from the comforters. They appear to be enmeshing themselves in the finer points of theology rather than identifying with Job as a human being. They appear not to have noticed the very agony of his suffering. Instead of responding to the points made by Bildad, therefore, Job instead concentrates on the intensity of his pains which are now increased by the comforters because, besides his physical suffering and the loss of his family, Job is also forced to suffer alone. His friends are actually adding to his suffering.

Only G-d can understand Job's suffering

The chapter opens with Job chastising the comforters for their lack of compassion.

How long will you distress my soul and oppress me with words?[124]

Job also questions from where they assume the authority to sit in judgement over him. How can they possibly know that he is a sinner?

And even if I have indeed sinned unwittingly, my error will come to rest with me.[125]

This verse is explained by Metzudath David[126] to mean that, even if Job were actually a sinner, only he would know it. Since they cannot know it, the comforters have no right at all to criticise him.

From this idea, modern scholars have suggested that perhaps ultimately the individual will always be given the opportunity to understand his/her personal suffering, although others may never do so. To use the modern example of the Nazi Holocaust, for example, those martyrs who perished in the concentration camps may themselves have understood why it was right for them to die at this time and in this way[127], but future generations may never understand it at all.

Job's criticism of the comforters at this point suggests that, whether or not the individual does understand his/her suffering, others must judge them favourably. The role of a comforter is to help the sufferer to cope, not to explain their suffering.

The injustice of G-d's treatment

For the rest of this chapter, Job ignores the comforters, who cannot give him answers, and turns his attention to the only one who can, G-d Himself. Job states that G-d has dealt with him unjustly [see v. 5]. The 'injustice' is not the suffering itself, however, but Job's inability to understand its purpose.

... I cry out... but I am not answered; I shout but there is no justice.[128]

This is not a blasphemy against G-d but a plea for clarity. Job wishes to understand his suffering in order to respond appropriately to it. Even though there is no response

124   Job 19:2
125   Job 19:4
126   Rabbi Yechiel Hillel Altschuller [18th century German commentary to Prophets].
127   There are many stories from Holocaust survivors of righteous men and women who went to their death in the gas chambers with a serene acceptance of their fate. See particularly 'The Unconquerable Spirit' [Artscroll 1980] which is a compilation of heroic tales from the Holocaust period.
128   Job 19: 7

from G-d at this point, the innate righteousness of Job is indicated.

> *He shatters me all about yet I go on...*[129]

Despite the lack of encouragement from any side, Job goes on, i.e. he continues to live a life of obedience and subservience to G-d. In this way, Job is the role model for those who do not understand why they are suffering. One must learn to be patient just like Job who, despite the bitterness in his heart and the complete lack of any answers at all, nevertheless continues to serve G-d and wait. Just as Job ultimately receives his answers, so will those who have the patience and accept G-d's decision not to share this information with us yet.

Job is shunned

In verses 13-22, Job cries out against the injustice of his friends and relatives, none of whom wish to have anything to do with him.

> *My colleagues look upon me with disgust; those that I loved have turned against me.*[130]

Job has been shunned because he is seen as one who is being punished by G-d. 'Decent people' therefore keep their distance. As mentioned previously, it is the responsibility of others to judge favourably and offer assistance, not to assume the worst. Job now turns to the comforters and pleads with them to show mercy.

> *... have pity on me my friends for the hand of G-d has afflicted me. Why do you [also] pursue me...*[131]

Is Job's pain not sufficient already that the comforters must add to it with their rejection him?

Job's faith that he will ultimately be vindicated

The chapter ends with Job expressing his belief that, despite everything that has happened to him, his suffering will eventually end and its purpose will be understood. This is indicated by Job referring to G-d as *My Redeemer* [v. 25], i.e. the One who will bring all this travail to an end.

---

129   Job 19:10
130   Job 19:19
131   Job 19:21-22

Most of the classical commentaries understand this [in line with the view that Job is a parable representing Israel's long exile] to be a message of consolation for the Jewish people. Despite the seemingly endless persecutions of the exile, they should not lose their belief in the ultimate deliverance when 'My Redeemer' will restore Israel to its former glory and all the acts of cruelty against the Jews throughout the generations will finally be understood.

This final passage also emphasises that answers will come only from G-d and not from Man. Ramban interprets this to mean that it is a folly for Israel to trust in a possible 'solution to the Jewish problem' coming from anywhere else. No new philosophy or political culture that the nations might embrace will free the world from anti-Semitism.

That will only come about through G-d's redemption at the end of the exile.[132]

---

132   It should be noted, however, that Rambam [Mishnah Torah: Hilchot Melachim 12] writes that it is possible that the nations will become so enlightened that the world will evolve into the Messianic Age. According to this, Job is not saying one must not trust in the goodness of humanity, but that the redemption is not dependant upon the goodness of humanity.

CHAPTER 38

G-D SPEAKS FROM THE WHIRLWIND

Job has heard all the comforters and has rejected all their explanations. Up to this point, all the explanations for suffering have been related in one form or another to the concept of retribution or punishment. There is a fourth comforter called Elihu who appears much later in the book (not part of our syllabus) who similarly fails to comfort Job in his suffering.

This does not mean that they were not accurately explaining why some people suffer, just that their answers were not relevant to Job. Instead of trying to relate Job's suffering to his personal circumstances, they start with a theory of why people suffer and try to fit Job's experience into that theory. This is Job's principal criticism of the comforters.

Job is suffering enormously, but he will not accept that his suffering is the consequence of his sins. This realisation does not lead him to reject G-d, but to turn to G-d for the answers that human beings have been unable to provide him.

It is very important to understand the response of Job since, according to the parable perspective of the book, Job represents any person whose suffering cannot be understood and he is the role model for others to emulate. Job is both honest and faithful. He turns to G-d with honesty because he does not understand why he is suffering. At the same time, however, he does not deny the justice of what is happening to him. He merely 'complains' that he does not understand why he is suffering. Job wants to know why he is suffering.

Job is completely confused. He does not know what is expected of him. If he cannot find the sin, what repentance is there to do? If there is no repentance to do, what is the appropriate response to his suffering? Some say that Job is identifying the very thin line that separates simple honesty from arrogance. Job is not arrogantly denying the justice of his suffering, but he is honestly expressing his bewilderment. Finally, therefore, Job's response is to 'challenge' G-d to give him an explanation for his suffering. In the last five chapters of the book, G-d does exactly this.

G-d challenges Job

G-d does not respond directly to the questions Job asks. Most commentaries agree that, by not dealing with the concept of retribution at all, G-d is actually pointing out that, in this case, retribution is not the issue. G-d does not supervise the world on a strictly 'cause and effect' basis. Whilst it might be true as a generality that the righteous are rewarded and the wicked are punished, the closer one examines the world the more clearly one is able to see just how many exceptions there are to this principle.

In Chapters 38-41, G-d appears to Job in a **storm theophany** (a harmonious fusion of all the most powerful forces of nature with G-d at the centre). In some translations, this is called a whirlwind. Instead of answering Job's questions, He quite surprisingly challenges him instead. So, instead of Job challenging G-d to explain Himself, it is G-d challenging Job to justify his question!

> *Where were you when I formed the earth? Speak up if you have understanding [of these matters].*[133]

Obviously, Job was not present at the time of the creation. G-d's rhetorical question emphasises **the impossibility of a mere human being fathoming the depths of G-d's wisdom.** This leads to the inevitable conclusion that, since G-d's wisdom is greater than human wisdom, there is no logic to any human being complaining that he does not understand G-d's actions. Job's question, therefore, is out of order.

Job is complaining that he does not understand why G-d is afflicting him with such suffering. But since it is impossible for Job (or anybody else) to understand G-d's actions anyway, he has no right to demand an answer to the question. In short, the question: Why is G-d doing this? is not a question to which one can automatically assume one will get an answer.

> *In all your days, did you ever command the morning [or] make known to the dawn its place?*[134]

According to Metzudath David, G-d is indicating to Job that He shows mercy to the world every day. The sun rises in such a way that its powerful rays are a benefit and a blessing for the world and not a cause of destruction. In similar fashion, G-d continues to detail the many aspects of the workings of the natural world, each example further emphasising the kindness He provides for the world constantly.

> *Can you hunt the prey for an old lion or supply the needs of the young lions?*[135]

---

133   Job 38:4
134   Job 38:12
135   Job 38:39

This kindness is not restricted to the inanimate world. Every living creature is provided with its needs. Those that cannot fend for themselves have assistance within 'nature' to ensure that their needs are met.

Who prepares sustenance for the raven when its chicks cry out G-d?[136]

Rashi points out that when ravens are hatched they are white and the parents [which are black] reject them and refuses to feed them. When the chicks cry out G-d causes small worms to grow from their dung and the chicks are sustained on these.

G-d continues to challenge Job to acknowledge His justice. The speech from the whirlwind continues to the end of Chapter 39. A further speech from the whirlwind, but of lesser intensity, follows in Chapters 40 and 41. This indicates that Job is beginning to rehabilitate but that he still has not completed the process. Rashi considers Job to have been convinced intellectually but not emotionally, i.e. he knew what G-d said was right but he still had not come to terms with his own suffering. By the end of Chapter 41, this process is completed.

---

136   Job 38:41

CHAPTER 42

G-D RESTORES EVERYTHING TO JOB

Chapter 42 can be divided into four sections:

1. JOB'S RESPONSE AND CONTRITION (v.1-6)

Job responds to G-d and acknowledges the power of G-d, whose purpose cannot be thwarted. Job admits that he has spoken of things he did not know and understand. Job then humbles himself before G-d in repentance.

> ... I can understand nothing; it is beyond me, I shall never know.[137]

In response to G-d's challenge to answer His questions, Job can only acknowledge that he has now seen G-d. From what he has now seen and heard, he realizes his error and repents. The very fact that G-d answers him at all, even if it is a rebuke, is a comfort.

Often, amidst the darkest persecutions, people received a fleeting indication of G-d's presence and that gave them the moral strength to persevere. They may never have understood why these horrific sufferings befell them, but just knowing that G-d is there is enough to restore one's trust and faith to continue in life.

2. G-D REBUKES THE COMFORTERS (v. 7-9)

With Job admitting he had spoken of things he did not understand and having repented, G-d now addresses Eliphaz as the representative of Job's three friends.

> My anger seethes against you... for you did not speak concerning Me appropriately as did My servant Job.[138]

They angered G-d by saying things that were not right about Him. This is not so much a rebuke of the comforters but a justification of Job in his rejection of their advice. Rashi states that what they said was not wrong in itself but it was not the comfort that Job needed. They are therefore instructed to offer seven bulls and seven rams and to trust that Job will pray on their behalf.

The comforters had erred, but they had erred unintentionally. It was appropriate, therefore, that they bring sin offerings, which atone for unintentional transgressions. The instruction to bring the sacrifices, therefore, is also a sign of G-d's acceptance of the comforters as well.

3. ALL IS RESTORED TO JOB (V. 10-11)

When Job has prayed for his friends, G-d begins to restore his losses. Job is comforted by his family and friends for the adversity that G-d has brought upon him. G-d then blesses Job by giving him twice the number of livestock he had in the beginning.

---

137   Job 42:3
138   Job 42:7

He is also blessed with seven sons and three daughters, the latter being named and described as the most beautiful in the land, even receiving an inheritance along with their brothers.

The fact that Job's fortunes change when he prays for the comforters is noted by the commentaries. Ibn Ezra suggests that, ultimately, pre-occupation with our own suffering is a form of self-indulgence. Awareness of the suffering of others gives us the strength to bear our own suffering which will now not look as bad as it did.

This could be an explanation of everything being restored to Job. Once he focused on the suffering of others, he had the strength to return to his life and 'restore' himself, in this case by succeeding again in business and having more children.

Ramban suggests that perhaps nothing was ever taken away from him in the first place! The original messengers in Chapter 1 were sent by the Satan to test Job. He believed their report, but never checked to see if it was true. Now that Job has been tested, it is revealed to him that he never lost either his business or his children. They were just concealed from him.

4. JOB IS BLESSED BY G-D (v. 12-17)

The book of Job closes with a mention of how Job lived another 140 years, seeing his descendants to the fourth generation before finally dying. There is a clear emphasis on the success of Job's life after the test. Some would deduce from here a comfort to the reader: all suffering will ultimately end and, when it does, the blessings will be greater than ever they were before.

We are left with a question concerning Job's children: were the original ones restored (Ramban) or were they replaced by a new family (Ibn Ezra)?

If we say they were replaced by a new family, then the message of the book is clear. Whatever we lose, if we respond positively to adversity, then G-d will give us the strength to replace it. But how can the birth of new children be a comfort for the children who died? Perhaps, the message is that, by having a new family, the pain of loss becomes more bearable.

If we say the original children were restored, then what is the message of the book? In real life, when tragedy strikes, the loss is permanent. Perhaps, it is an indication that there is a world after this one in which all the losses will be restored to us. The message then would be that, in truth, this world can appear to be unjust and unfair. We can only cope with our suffering if we are comforted by our belief in an after-life where the righteous do receive their just reward.

So why did Job suffer?

If we go back to the beginning of the book, we will remember that Job had not, in fact, committed any sins at all. The Satan wanted to test Job to ascertain if his righteousness would withstand his tests. Job is never told this, even at the end of the book. Why is this information withheld?

Perhaps it was not necessary to tell Job! Job understood that life was a series of tests and that all tests are opportunities for growth. He would have intuitively understood that, when he was finally vindicated, no mention was made of any sins that had brought about his suffering. His suffering was therefore a test, an opportunity for growth. When G-d communicated with him it asserted the nature of his suffering.

What exactly the test was for, the details of where it came from, this is not revealed, but this is not important. G-d never sets a test that a human being cannot pass. That is a lesson of the book. It is enough to know that G-d is testing us because that, in itself, is the guarantee that one can 'pass' the tests of tragedy and sadness that every human being has to cope with.

THEMES FROM JEWISH SCRIPTURES:

G-D &

SUFFERING

THE BOOK OF JONAH

WITH PARTICULAR REFERENCE TO:

- THE UNIQUE NATURE OF THE BOOK
- ITS PARTICULAR TEACHINGS ABOUT THE NATURE OF G-D
- ITS UNDERSTANDING OF THE NATURE OF THE SUFFERING OF THE JEWS

PARTICULAR REFERENCE MUST BE MADE TO THE THEMES OF:

- OBEDIENCE
- THE INABILITY TO HIDE FROM G-D OR RESIST G-D'S WISHES
- THE RELATIONSHIP WITH NON-JEWS

INTRODUCTION

Jonah is the fifth of the Twelve Minor Prophets, the fourth and final book of the Later Prophets. Unlike the other prophetic books in this section, the book of Jonah contains only one short prophecy.[139] The rest of the book is a story which, according to Orthodox tradition, is an historical narrative. The book is divided into four chapters, whose content can be briefly summarised as follows:

Chapter One: In the boat

Jonah is instructed by G-d to go to Nineveh and proclaim judgment upon its people for their wickedness. He refuses to fulfill the mission and tries to escape. At Jaffa he boards a ship bound for Tarshish, a direction precisely opposite to Nineveh. G-d brings on a great storm. The sailors try to avert the danger by praying to their idols and throwing their vessels overboard. Jonah, who has gone to sleep, is awakened by the captain who asks him too to pray to his G-d. The sailors then decide to find out by casting lots on whose account this misfortune has come upon them. The lot falls on Jonah, and they try to find out what wrong he has done. Jonah discloses that he is fleeing from a mission of G-d and that the only way they can end the storm is by throwing him overboard. The sailors first try to row back to land but when this proves futile they throw Jonah overboard and pray to G-d not to hold them guilty for his murder, since it was He who left them no other way of saving themselves. The storm subsides at once and the sailors, who now greatly fear G-d, offer sacrifices and make vows.

---

139   *... in another forty days Nineveh shall be overturned.* [3:4]

Chapter Two: In the fish

Jonah himself is swallowed by a great fish, from inside of which he prays to G-d and repents of his actions. After three days and nights in the fish's stomach he is vomited out onto dry land.

Chapter Three: In Nineveh

Jonah is called by G-d a second time to bring His message to Nineveh. This time Jonah does go to Nineveh, a huge city. He proclaims that in 40 days Nineveh will be overthrown. The people of Nineveh believe God, proclaim a fast and put on sackcloth. The king of Nineveh also participates in the acts of repentance and orders all the inhabitants to pray to G-d and to repent of their evil ways. As a result of Nineveh's repentance, G-d revokes the punishment He had planned to bring upon it.

Chapter Four: The kikayon

Jonah is greatly displeased by this mercy and complains of it to G-d. He had tried to escape his mission in the first place for fear that G-d would be moved to renounce His punishment out of mercy. In his frustration, Jonah asks G-d to take his life. At this time Jonah is outside Nineveh sitting in the shade of a booth waiting to see what will happen to the city. G-d causes a kikayon [a very large plant] to grow unexpectedly over Jonah to provide shade over his head, to his great relief. On the following day, however, G-d sends a worm, which attacks the plant causing it to wither. When the sun rises, G-d causes a hot east wind to beat down on Jonah's head. Jonah becomes faint and asks for death. Then G-d says: "You cared about the plant, which you did not work for and which you did not grow, which appeared overnight and perished overnight. And should I not care about Nineveh, that great city, in which there are more than a hundred and twenty thousand persons who do not yet know their right hand from their left, and many beasts as well?"

What is the Central Message of the Book?

There are a number of religious concepts identifiable in this book:

Repentance: The sailors repent of their idolatry, the Ninevites repent of their cruelty and Jonah repents of refusing to deliver his prophecy. This is why the book of Jonah is recited as the Haftorah at the afternoon service [Minchah] on Yom Kippur. But if repentance was the central theme there would be no need for the last chapter.

G-d's concern for Gentiles: Another message is that sincere repentance is accepted from non-Jews [sailors, Ninevites] as well as from Jews. The fact that the Jews are the Chosen People does not give them a monopoly on G-d's care and compassion. But if this was the central theme we would have to wonder why this lesson was specifically taught through the Ninevites. We would also wonder why Jonah was so reluctant to deliver it.

Free will: Jonah seems to have his free will interfered with. He apparently has no choice but to go to Nineveh. Yet G-d created Man with free-will. That is his specific defining feature as no other creature was given free-will. There must be some lesson here about the nature of free-will.

In order to discover the central message of the book, however, we must first consider its historical context.

WHO

WAS

JONAH?

The period of Israel's settlement in the land can be divided into three:

First period: From Joshua's conquest until the death of King Solomon, when all twelve tribes were united into one sovereign kingdom.

Second period: Following Solomon's death, the kingdom split in two: the kingdom of Israel, comprising the ten northern tribes; the kingdom of Judea comprising the tribes of Judah and Benjamin. This period continued until the Assyrian conquest and exile of the northern kingdom.

Third period: The continued survival of the southern kingdom of Judea until the Babylonian conquest and destruction of the First temple.

According to the Biblical record, Jonah lived during the penultimate generation of the second period. This period is described in the second half of I Kings and in the first half of II Kings. Jonah is actually mentioned by name in the second book of Kings:

> _...Jeroboam son of Yoash king of Israel ruled Samaria forty years. ... He restored Israel's boundary... according to the word of G-d... which He spoke through His servant Jonah son of Amittai...[140]_

Jonah was a prophet to the Northern kingdom of Israel during the reign of Jeroboam II. According to Seder Olam, Jeroboam's reign began in 646BCE. Jonah is also identified[141] as the servant of Elisha who anointed a previous king, Jehu, an event charted by Seder Olam as taking place in 706 BCE. This would identify Jonah as a prophet who lived at the end of the eighth and the through the first half of the seventh century BCE.

No specific mention is made of when the events in the book of Jonah took place, but it is reasonable to assume that it was some time during the first half of the seventh century BCE.

140   **_II Kings 14:23-25_**
141   **_See Rashi and ReDaK commentaries to II Kings 10:30_**

This coincides with the generally accepted dates for the domination of the Assyrian empire which, according to archeological findings, rose to prominence around 670 BCE and remained a major force until its conquest by the Babylonians. It was during this period that Assyria conquered and exiled the Northern Kingdom.

In Jewish tradition, Jonah is understood to have been one of the many prophets sent to warn the Northern Kingdom that, unless they repented and forsook their evil ways, their kingdom would be destroyed and they would be exiled from the land.

The people ignored Jonah's warnings and this caused him great anguish. His anguish was not because his honour had been slighted but because he was so concerned for what would happen to the people if they continued to ignore him. The Midrashim on Jonah emphasise this. They point out that Jonah's principal character trait was his intense love for the people and the thought of their suffering was very painful to him.

Jonah lived at a time when the Assyrian empire was becoming stronger and stronger. Eventually, under the emperor Sanncheriv, the Assyrians would conquer the northern kingdom and send the ten tribes into exile. The capital of the Assyrian empire was Nineveh, the city to which Jonah was sent to deliver his prophecy.

WHEN WAS THE BOOK OF JONAH WRITTEN?

There is no evidence at all to suggest that Jonah wrote his own book.

The Talmud[142] records the tradition that the Twelve Minor Prophets is actually one book compiled and edited by the Men of the Great Assembly during the early Second Temple period. Jonah may well have recorded this story among all his prophecies, but the form in which we have the story now is probably an edited form dating from the fourth century BCE.

Studies in Form Criticism have attempted to suggest an even later date. This is because its literary style emphases G-d's care for the non-Jews of Nineveh. This led Christian scholars to understand its message to be that Israel would one day be rejected as the Chosen People! This idea is problematical, however, as the book of Jonah is mentioned in the Apocryphal work Ben Sira, which is itself dated by Form Criticism in the third century BCE.

The Talmudic conclusion, consequently, does seem the most reasonable.

---

142   *Bava Bathra 14b-15a*

SO WHAT IS

THE CENTRAL MESSAGE

OF THE BOOK?

Jonah was primarily a prophet to the Northern Kingdom. The purpose of all Jonah's prophecies at this time was to warn of the impending destruction and exile at the hands of the Assyrians. The book of Jonah, therefore, must be connected to this theme. The original message of the book, consequently, must have been to warn that this destruction and exile was much closer than anybody realised.

Problems in the book of Jonah

A superficial reading of this book throws up a number of questions. It is by answering these questions that the real message of the book comes to light.

1) How can somebody run away from G-d?

When G-d tells Jonah to go to Nineveh, he attempts to run away from G-d. Even the simplest person knows that G-d is everywhere, so it is impossible to run away from Him. Surely someone considered great enough to be given prophecy also knew this! So why did Jonah run away?

2) Where Is Jonah's free-will?

If Jonah was eventually forced by G-d to do what He wanted, then Jonah did not have free-will. How can G-d remove Jonah's free-will?

3) Why did G-d send a Jewish prophet a prophecy for a non-Jewish nation?

This is the one and only occasion in the Bible where a Jewish prophet is sent from Israel to non-Jews with a prophecy. What was so special about Nineveh that G-d chose to do this?

4) What is the significance of the sailors?

The storm at sea was to punish Jonah, so why did the sailors have to suffer as well? We have to examine what role the sailors play in this story.

5) Was Jonah really swallowed by a fish?

The Talmud explains that no miracles occur in the Tenach unless they are absolutely necessary. G-d does not need to impress us with magic tricks. What is the point of this part of the story?

6) Why did the King of Nineveh respond so positively to Jonah's warning?

It is unusual for a leader to accept the word of someone from another country so easily, especially if it is a country he is planning to conquer!

7) What is the message of the Kikayon?

What lesson was G-d trying to get across to Jonah by way of this miraculous plant?

Chapter One

In
the
boat

1 Now the word of G-d came to Jonah the son of Amittai, saying: 2 'Arise, go to Nineveh, that great city, and proclaim against it; for their wickedness has come up before Me.' 3 But Jonah arose to flee to Tarshish from the presence of G-d; and he went down to Jaffa, and he found a ship going to Tarshish; so he paid its fare and went down into it to go with them to Tarshish from the presence of G-d. 4 But G-d hurled a great wind into the sea and there was a mighty storm in the sea, so that the ship was likely to be broken. 5 And the sailors were afraid, and cried each man to his god; and they cast off their vessels that were in the ship into the sea, to lighten it, but Jonah had gone down into the innermost parts of the ship; and he lay, and was fast asleep. 6 So the captain came to him and said to him: 'Why do you sleep? Arise, call upon your G-d, so that G-d will consider us, that we perish not.' 7 And they said to each other: 'Come, and let us cast lots, that we may know on whose account this evil is upon us;' so they cast lots, and the lot fell upon Jonah. 8 Then they said to him: 'Tell us why this evil has befallen us: what is your occupation and where do you come from; what is your country and of what people are you?' 9 And he said to them: 'I am an Ivri [Hebrew] and I fear G-d, the G-d of heaven, who has made the sea and the dry land.' 10 Then the men were very afraid, and said to him: 'What is this that you have done?' for the men knew that he had fled from the presence of G-d, because he had told them. 11 Then they said to him: 'What shall we do to you that the sea may be calm for us?' for the sea grew more and more stormy. 12 And he said to them: 'Take me up and cast me out into the sea; then shall the sea be calm for you for I know that it is on account of me that this great storm is upon you.' 13 Nevertheless the men rowed hard to bring it to the land but they could not for the sea grew more and more stormy against them. 14 Then they cried out to G-d and said: 'We beseech You, O G-d, we beseech You, let us not perish for this man's life and lay not upon us innocent blood for you O G-d have done as it pleased You.' 15 So they took up Jonah, and cast him out into the sea and the sea ceased from its raging. 16 Then the men feared G-d exceedingly; and they offered a sacrifice to G-d, and made vows

Why did G-d give this prophecy to Jonah?

This is the only occasion in the Tenach when a Jewish prophet is instructed to encourage a non-Jewish nation to repent. Jonah realises immediately that this instruction must have a connection to the conduct of Israel, otherwise a Jewish prophet would not have been selected for this mission.

Ever since attaining the level of prophecy, Jonah's life had been dedicated to warning the Northern Kingdom that they must desist from wickedness or face conquest and exile from the land. Since the Assyrian empire was the strongest force at that time, Jonah realised that, if Israel was to be conquered, it would be the Assyrians who would conquer them.

Since Nineveh was the capital of Assyria, it was clear to Jonah that this mission was connected to a possible Assyrian conquest. If the Assyrians listened to Jonah and changed their ways, they would have a spiritual advantage over Israel who had ignored Jonah's warnings. This would give the Assyrians the spiritual superiority necessary to defeat Israel in battle.

Why did Jonah run away?

We can now understand why Jonah ran away. He was not running away from G-d, for he knew that that was impossible. He was running away from the prophecy. The Talmud explains that (apart from Moses) no other prophet was able to receive prophecy outside Israel. Jonah reasoned that if he left Israel, G-d would not be able to instruct him, the warning would not be given to Nineveh and Israel would not be conquered. Since Nineveh is north-east of Israel, he set out in a south-westerly direction.

This actually highlights the righteousness of Jonah. Jonah was aware of the Torah law that a prophet who fails to bring his message to the people is liable to death. His love of his people was so great, however, that he would rather allow G-d to kill him than do something that would ultimately bring harm on the people. This also introduces us to Jonah's first mistake.

What was Jonah's first mistake?

Jonah's actions demonstrate a misunderstanding of punishment. It says in Ethics of the Fathers: the reward for a mitzvah is a mitzvah and the reward (i.e. consequence) of a transgression is a transgression. This means that the greatest benefit from doing a mitzvah is not the reward but the reality of having done the mitzvah. The advantage of having done the mitzvah is its own reward. Similarly, the loss entailed in transgression is far greater than any punishment.

Example: *A teacher sets her class homework and says that those who don't do the homework will have a lunchtime detention. The real 'punishment' for not doing the homework is not having the knowledge that would have been gained by doing it. The point of the teacher saying there will be a detention is to deter the children from not doing their homework. The child who calculates that it would not be so bad to have a detention so they don't do the homework suffers far more from the undone homework than from the detention.*

When a choice of action is presented in which Choice A will receive a reward and Choice B will receive a punishment, consequently, the purpose of the reward and punishment is merely to encourage the selection of Choice A. The punishment is never intended to be used. It is only a deterrent and is not in reality a punishment at all. Jonah chose the transgression and the storm that follows was intended to teach Jonah the nature of his mistake.

Why did Jonah head for Tarshish?

Jonah arose and fled from the presence of G-d. He intended to escape to Tarshish and went down to Jaffa where he found a ship bound for Tarshish. Jaffa was Israel's main sea-port at that time, so it was the most obvious place to go if you wanted to travel west in a hurry. Tarshish was a popular destination for merchants selling their wares abroad. Most commentaries identify it with a port in southern Spain, but others say it was in northern Turkey.

What fare did Jonah pay?

It says that Jonah paid its fare (v.3) rather than his fare. This implies that Jonah paid whatever was necessary for the boat to leave immediately. This fits both with Jonah being in a hurry and the fact that there do not seem to be any other passengers on the boat, a most unusual occurrence for a cargo boat.

Why were the sailors afraid?

Once the boat was out at sea, G-d brought a strong wind which became so fearsome that it looked like the boat would be wrecked. The sailors were afraid and each one cried out to his god. They then threw their vessels overboard to lighten it. Storms at sea are not unusual. It is from this statement that the Rabbis deduce that it was a supernatural storm, one so strange that even hardened sailors were terrified. They explain that, in an otherwise completely calm sea, there was one cloud directly over their boat and it was raining down incessantly upon it. Wherever the boat moved, the cloud moved with it!

Why did the sailors pray first and throw their vessels away afterwards?

In normal circumstances, with the advent of a storm the sailors would first lighten the ship and only when all else had failed would they start praying. Here, they pray first. This also suggests a supernatural storm that immediately had the sailors quaking in fear.

What did the sailors throw overboard?

Again, the Rabbis were puzzled by this. After all, we have already established that there were no other passengers aboard but Jonah, who brought nothing with him. There was no cargo to throw overboard! They conclude that the 'vessels' referred to were their idols. They had each prayed to their idols and now realised that their idols were powerless to help them so they threw them away.

Why was Jonah not concerned about the storm?

Jonah meanwhile had gone down into his cabin and lay down and slept. The captain discovered him and admonished him. He asked why he was sleeping and not calling out to his god like everybody else?

Jonah, of course, thought he knew exactly what was happening. He had committed a capital crime and G-d was now going about the process of putting him to death. Jonah went to lay down because he was completely at peace with the situation. He had accepted death as the consequence of his actions and was ready to take his punishment. This also highlights the moral integrity of Jonah. He had done something wrong and was willing to accept the consequences of his actions. Jonah's answer to the captain is not recorded. Presumably, he did not 'call out to his god' as there was no point, as explained.

Why did the sailors draw lots?

Realising they were getting no 'assistance' from Jonah, the sailors now decided to draw lots to ascertain who was responsible for the storm. It could be asked: why should they suspect the cause of the storm was to be found on their ship? Again, the above interpretation of the Rabbis that the storm was only directed at their ship would provide the answer!

The method of casting lots is not specified nor is it significant. The plural form is used, suggesting that different methods were used, but no matter how the lot was cast it always selected Jonah. The sailors were now convinced (correctly!) that the storm was on account of Jonah. They approached him and demanded that he tell them why he was punished so, what was his trade, where did he come from and of which nation. Jonah answered that he was an Ivri (English: Hebrew) who had fled from the presence of G-d.

Jonah call himself an Ivri?

Why did Jonah use just this word to describe himself? Why did he not say that he was from Israel or that he was an Israelite?

The word Ivri is derived from the Hebrew verb la'avor, which means to cross over. This word was first used to describe Abraham because, according to the Talmud, the whole world believed in one thing, i.e. idolatry and Abraham 'crossed over' to a different belief, i.e. monotheism. The word Ivri continued to be associated with monotheism and was used to identify Israel when the intention was to emphasise the fact that they were the only monotheistic nation. Jonah's self-definition as Ivri, consequently, not only told the sailors just who he was but also answered the only question that they really wanted an answer for: the storm was being brought by the G-d of Israel as a punishment of him.

This answer increased the fear of the sailors. At this point in history, approximately eight hundred years had passed since Joshua had led the Israelites across the River Jordan to begin the conquest of the seven nations. In all that time, although Israel had lost occasional battles and suffered temporary setbacks, not one nation had ever succeeded in conquering and ruling over Israel. In the minds of the sailors, this meant that the G-d of Israel was so much more powerful than all the other gods. That is why their fear increased at this point. They realised just what they were up against!

Why didn't the sailors want to throw Jonah overboard?

They asked him what they should do with him to make the sea calm for them. Jonah replied that they should throw him into the sea for they only suffered a storm because he was with them. They were afraid to do this, however, since he had told them he was a prophet. Whatever he may have done wrong, he was someone that G-d communicates with and so they were reluctant to do him harm. If this is how G-d punishes His prophet for his crime, how much more would He punish them for murdering His prophet!!!

Why didn't Jonah jump in the sea himself?

Jonah was only willing to break the law in order to help his people. He would not go against G-d's commands in any other circumstance. Throwing himself overboard would be an act of suicide for, in normal circumstances, it is impossible to survive in the middle of the ocean. On the other hand, the sailors were halachically permitted to throw him overboard in order to save their own lives, as is explained in the following passage from the Talmud:

> A town was besieged by a hostile army. Their leader called out that if they sent out a certain person (who they wanted to put to death) they would lift their siege and spare the town. If they refused, then they would kill them all. The Rabbis were consulted and gave the following ruling: if the wanted person had committed a crime for which Torah law condemns him to death, then they are permitted to hand him over in order to save themselves; if not, then they must refuse.

Jonah reasoned that, since he had committed a capital crime, the sailors were permitted to throw him overboard in order to save their own lives. The Talmud also records that Jonah saw drowning as a fitting death penalty for his crime. Since he suppressed his prophecy (refused to open his mouth), he will die a death that removes his ability to breathe.

The sailors tried to row harder in order to bring the ship back to the shore, but the harder they rowed the stronger the storm raged. Some say the storm was coming from the direction of the shore, thus forcing them to row further and further away. In their desperation they now cry out to G-d that they not be punished for shedding the blood of this man for it was not their wish but G-d's doing that was the cause of all this. They then took hold of Jonah and cast him into the sea. Immediately, the storm ceased.

The commentaries point out that this was the first time these sailors had ever prayed to G-d. Previously, they had prayed to their own idols and there had been no response. Now they pray to G-d and get an immediate positive answer. This was to have a profound effect upon them, as shall be shown.

How did the sailors respond to this miracle?

The sailors now feared G-d greatly, offered sacrifices and made vows. When the sailors digested the awesomeness of what they had just seen, they were overcome with fear of G-d. The commentaries identify this response as positive not negative. Some say that they were so overwhelmed by G-d's power that they immediately committed themselves to convert to Judaism. According to this interpretation, their sacrifices were sin offerings that had to be brought as part of the conversion process and their vows were vows of commitment to observe the laws of the Torah.

Others say they committed themselves to becoming righteous gentiles. Their sacrifices were thanksgiving offerings for being brought back safely to shore and their vows were vows of commitment to observe the seven Noahide laws binding on all non-Jews.

Conclusion to Chapter One

The storm incident indicates the greatness of G-d's justice. Human justice only considers the crime and the individual, but Divine justice can take everybody into account, e.g. if a man robs a bank, a court may find him guilty and send him to jail. That is human justice. It is just for the man to go to jail, but why should his wife and children be punished by the loss of their husband and father for so many years? Divine justice, by contrast, is just to everybody. The same action which serves to punish Jonah at the same time has a positive effect on the sailors and is directly responsible for their forsaking idolatry.

The incident of the sailors also indicates how G-d influences, but crucially does not remove, a person's free-will. The sailors were only idolaters because, in the environment that they had come from, they knew no other form of worship. By subjecting them to a supernatural storm, G-d was presenting them with the opportunity of increasing their knowledge and experience. The sailors were given the means to forsake idolatry and embrace monotheism if they chose to do so, but it always remained their choice.

Similarly, at every stage Jonah also had free-will. He was, or so he thought, choosing to die for what he believed to be right. He was free to fulfill G-d's commands or take the consequences of going against them. It was always his choice.

Chapter Two

In
the
fish

1 And G-d prepared a great fish to swallow up Jonah; and Jonah was in the belly of the fish three days and three nights. 2 Then Jonah prayed to G-d, his G-d, out of the fish's belly. 3 And he said: I called out of my affliction to G-d and He answered me; out of the belly of the deep I cried out and You heard my voice. 4 For You cast me into the deep, into the heart of the sea and the flood surrounded me; all Your waves and Your storm passed over me. 5 And I said: 'I am cast out from before Your eyes'; yet I will look again toward Your holy Temple. 6 The waters encompassed me about, even to the soul; the deep was round about me; the weeds were wrapped about my head. 7 I went down to the bottoms of the mountains; the earth with her bars closed upon me for ever; yet have You brought up my life from the pit, O G-d, my G-d. 8 When my soul fainted within me, I remembered G-d; and my prayer came to You, into Your holy Temple. 9 They that guard worthless vanities forsake their own kindness. 10 But as for me, I will bring offerings to You with the voice of gratitude; that which I have vowed I will pay; salvation is of G-d. 11 And G-d spoke to the fish and it vomited Jonah out upon the dry land.

Why is Jonah still alive?

Now G-d had appointed a great fish to swallow up Jonah. He was in the belly of the fish for three days and three nights and cried out to G-d. At this point, Jonah began to think about his situation. He thought that he was a deliberate transgressor of a crime that carried a death penalty, i.e. failing to deliver the prophecy of G-d. If that were so, then he would have drowned in the sea. Why did G-d save him from death by having a fish swallow him?

Jonah realised that he must have made some kind of mistake. If he was an accidental transgressor, then G-d would give him the opportunity to realise his mistake and repent. If the repentance was sincere, then G-d would forgive him.

What did Jonah think was his mistake?

The Talmud states that Jonah compared himself to Abraham at the time he was commanded to offer Isaac as a sacrifice. Abraham did not understand why G-d would want him to do this, for it contradicted everything he knew about G-d (that He abhorred human sacrifice) and about the future (for G-d had promised to make a great nation out of his descendants, but the still unmarried Isaac was his only descendant) but Abraham nevertheless believed in the intrinsic rightness of G-d's commands and was prepared to do it anyway even if, according to his logic, it was a disastrous thing to do.

In the same way, Jonah had been asked to do something which also seemed, to his logic, to be a disastrous thing to do. If the people of Nineveh accepted his warning and repented, then they would have a spiritual advantage over Israel which would lead to Israel's conquest and exile. If the people of Nineveh ignored his warning and nothing happened to them (for how many times had Israel been warned and nothing, as yet, had happened to them) then the Ninevites would ridicule him as a false prophet and the name of G-d would be desecrated.

Jonah now cries out to G-d that he realises he should have obeyed G-d's command and trusted in the intrinsic rightness of G-d's commands just as Abraham had done. Perhaps, just as Abraham never had to sacrifice Isaac in the end, some as yet unknown outcome will also happen in his case. In Chapter Three, when Jonah finally goes to Nineveh, the narrative uses the same Hebrew expression '...and [he] arose...and he went' (3:3) as is used to describe Abraham setting out for the mountain with Isaac (see Genesis 22:3).

Which fish swallowed Jonah?

We do not know and it does not really matter. The point of the narrative is that G-d performed a miracle by which a human being was able to live inside a fish. In a natural way, this is completely impossible. According to Maimonides, this particular event never happened!! When Jonah was thrown overboard, he fell into a state of unconsciousness and dreamed that he was swallowed by a fish. When he awoke, he had been miraculously washed ashore.

The process of repentance

Maimonides also writes that the narrative of Jonah's prayer inside the fish is a principal source in Judaism for understanding how to repent:

The first stage is confession, i.e. to admit that you have done something wrong.

The second stage is remorse, i.e. to regret and feel very bad about doing wrong. This does not mean feeling bad about being caught or about being punished, but about having done something you should not have done.

The third stage is resolution, i.e. the sincere desire not to do this ever again. Included in this stage is a plan of action to take precautions against ever doing this again. It is not enough to just have good intentions, there has to be a proper strategy as well.

Finally, the fourth stage is being in the same situation again and not doing wrong this time. In this chapter, Jonah's prayer includes the first three stages. Jonah is presented with the fourth stage at the beginning of the next chapter.

Conclusion to Chapter Two

Besides the principles of repentance, this chapter also emphasises the extent of G-d's mercy. If a person does something wrong, the punishment will be cancelled if it is clear that, had they fully appreciated all the consequences of what they were doing, they would not have done it. Repentance is the means by which the sinner demonstrates to G-d that His mercy was not misplaced.

This also explains why it is that some people sin and are not punished. Only G-d knows their innermost thoughts. Perhaps they did not fully realise that what they were doing was wrong. Perhaps, had they understand this, they would never have done it in the first place. Sometimes, G-d gives people the chance to find out and the opportunity to regret their deeds. If their regret is sincere then the sin is erased completely.

Alternatively, of course, a person may be given the opportunity to repent and not take the opportunity. In this case, the opportunity to repent was a second chance which was not taken and so the punishment will now be reinstated.

Chapter Three:

In

Nineveh

1 And the word of G-d came to Jonah a second time, saying. 2 'Arise, go to Nineveh, that great city, and make the proclamation which I say to you.' 3 So Jonah arose and went to Nineveh, according to the word of G-d'; now Nineveh was a very large city, of three days' journey. 4 And Jonah entered into the city a day's journey, and proclaimed, and said: 'In another forty days Nineveh shall be overthrown.' 5 And the people of Nineveh believed in G-d; they proclaimed a fast and put on sackcloth, from the greatest of them to the least of them. 6 And word reached the king of Nineveh; he arose from his throne and removed his robe, covered himself with sackcloth and sat in ashes. 7 And he caused it to be proclaimed and published through Nineveh by the decree of the king and his nobles, saying: 'Let neither man nor beast, herd nor flock, taste anything; let them not graze or drink water. 8 But let them be covered with sackcloth, both man and beast, and let them cry mightily to G-d; let them turn every one from his evil way, and from the robbery that is in their hands. 9 He who knows, let him repent and G-d may relent and turn away from His fierce anger, that we perish not.' 10 And G-d saw their deeds, that they turned from their evil ways, and so G-d relented of the calamity which He said He would do to them and He did it not.

The completion of Jonah's repentance

The commentaries point out that the wording at the beginning of Chapter Three is almost identical to the wording at the beginning of Chapter One. This indicates the fourth and final stage of the repentance process. Jonah is placed in the identical position in which he first did wrong and given the opportunity to this time do the right thing.

By saying that Jonah did everything ...according to the word of G-d... (v.3) indicates that the repentance process was now complete and Jonah's original transgression was now erased. The opening verses of this chapter, therefore, are a praise of Jonah's actions.

Why were the Ninevites given forty days to repent?

The number forty is associated with repentance, punishment and transition in many places in Tenach.

The period of repentance for the worshipping of the golden calf (from Rosh Chodesh Ellul until Yom Kippur) lasted forty days and that is also the period of repentance for all Jews each year.
The punishment of the flood lasted forty days.
The punishment for the generation of the wilderness lasted forty years.

There are forty weeks from a baby's conception until its birth, representing the transition from foetus to human.

Similarly, the people of Nineveh are given forty days to repent and effect a transformation or to fail to repent and receive a punishment.

Why did the Ninevites respond so positively?

Some say that the sailors also went to Nineveh and told the people of the miraculous storm. When they heard about G-d's power, they were so frightened of His punishment that they immediately begged Him for mercy. When it says that they believed in G-d, it means that they believed He had the power to destroy them and they were afraid of Him.

Others say that the influence of the king was all-important. The initial fear of the people at first was sufficient to motivate many of them to fast and wear sackcloth. The king's decree guaranteed that all the people did this. It also taught them that outward gestures of remorse were not enough. They also had to forsake their evil and cruel way of life.

According to both interpretations, the repentance of the Ninevites was inferior to the repentance of the sailors. The Ninevites repented only out of fear of punishment. The sailors, however, recognised that G-d was the only power in the universe and chose to worship Him because that that was the right thing to do.

Why was it necessary for the animals to fast?

Some say this was a further act of penance for the people. Animals were used either for work or for food. If they did not eat they would not be able to work as efficiently or they would have less meat or produce less milk. In all cases, this would lead to economic hardship for the people. Similarly, the horses of the wealthy, which were usually covered with attractive, distinctive designs, were to be covered in sackcloth.

Why did the king respond positively to the prophecy?

A Midrashic commentary[143] states that the king of Nineveh was Pharaoh, the same Pharaoh who had been subjected to the ten plagues and seen his army destroyed in the Red Sea. Having been spared at that time, he had eventually ended up in Nineveh where he became the king. When he heard that another Israelite prophet was warning of the G-d of Israel's intention to punish his people, he remembered the catastrophes he suffered in Egypt and did not try to fight against G-d again. This is another example of the fourth and final stage of repentance.

In Egypt, Pharaoh had failed to listen to Moses, the Israelite prophet. Now another Israelite prophet was giving him another warning. Pharaoh, as king of Nineveh, was being put in the same situation again. This time he did the right thing, thus completing his process of repentance for the ten plagues and for chasing the Israelites into the Red Sea.

---

143   *Pirkei D'Rebbe Eliezer:43*

The lesson of this Midrash is that nobody, not even someone as wicked as Pharaoh, who was responsible for enslaving the entire Jewish people, is too wicked to repent. Nobody should ever 'give up on themselves' for sincere repentance is always accepted, even following the most wicked actions. If even Pharaoh's repentance is accepted, there is hope for everybody.

Is this Midrash meant to be taken literally?

Not every Midrashic tale is a true story. Some are parables invented to teach important lessons. It is sometimes very difficult to tell which Midrashim are historical and which are parables. If we take this Midrash literally, then Pharaoh lived for many centuries. Many Torah scholars find this difficult to accept. There are two alternative explanations.

Perhaps it was a descendant of Pharaoh who became the king of Nineveh. In that case, the message of the Midrash would be that, if a person truly regrets his actions, even if he is no longer able to be placed in the same position again in his lifetime, then the final stage of repentance can be accomplished by a descendant. For example, suppose a person lived a very wicked life but, whilst on his deathbed sincerely repented and warned his children not to follow in his ways. His children would then be placed in the same situation that he had been and, due to his warning, they do not sin, then it is considered as if he himself had been in that situation and he is accredited with having achieved the fourth stage of repentance.

Alternatively, perhaps the story is a complete parable and the king of Nineveh was not a descendant of Pharaoh at all. In that case, the message of the Midrash would be the same, only the Rabbis used the book of Jonah as a vehicle for teaching this message.

Why did G-d accept their repentance?

The chapter concludes by stating that when G-d saw their deeds, that they had turned back from their evil ways, He chose not to bring destruction upon them. The Talmud[144] emphasises that it was not their fasting or sackcloth that brought about their salvation, but the fact that they had changed their deeds.

---

144   *Taanit 16a*

Conclusion to Chapter Three

There are number of ideas concerning the nature of repentance that can be deduced from the narrative of this chapter:

- o although there is a difference between the way G-d treats Jews and non-Jews (see below), nevertheless **sincere repentance is accepted from all**;

- o prayer and remorse are not sufficient preparatory acts for repentance, **fasting** is also required;

- o it says G-d saw their deeds (v.10) indicating that the purpose of the repentance process is that **a person must change their actions and become a better person**;

- o it is also pointed out that the Ninevites only changed their deeds in respect to cruelty to each other, but that they continued to worship idols; this indicates **that G-d, in His mercy, rewards even a partial improvement** and a person should not be discouraged from self-improvement just because he cannot change all his bad ways.

This chapter is also one of the sources for the Talmudic maxim that **all prophecies that something bad will happen are conditional**. Sincere repentance and the forsaking of the unacceptable behaviour will always prevent the prophecy from coming true. A prophecy, therefore, never removes a person's free-will.

G-d responds differently to non-Jews

The Talmud explains that, as a consequence of the selection of the Chosen People, **there is a difference between the way G-d relates to Israel and to all other nations.** G-d made a promise to Abraham that his descendants would never be destroyed. This means that G-d will interfere with nature in order to ensure Israel's survival. If Israel sins, G-d will punish them immediately so that the sin will be atoned for and the people will never descend to the spiritual level at which they will cease to exist. This is one explanation for why the Jews have been persecuted so much in every generation.

With Gentiles, this is not the case. They will certainly be rewarded for all the good they do, as the Talmud states that the righteous of all nations have a portion in the next world. If they live sinfully however, they will not be punished immediately. If they sincerely regret their actions and repent, their repentance will be accepted the same as with Israel. If not, when they reached the lowest spiritual level, they will be removed from the world entirely, either by conquest or by assimilation into another nation.

The only exception to this process is in this book. G-d did not send a prophet to Nineveh because He wanted to give the Ninevites a unique opportunity to repent, for that would contradict the way He deals with all the other Gentile nations. After all, why should He show special concern for Nineveh? Rather, He wanted to punish Israel (the Northern Kingdom) with exile and so He arranged for the capital of Assyria to have the spiritual superiority that would enable it to defeat and exile the Northern Kingdom.

Chapter Four

The Kikayon

1 But it displeased Jonah exceedingly and he was angry. 2 And he prayed to G-d and said: 'Please G-d, was not this my contention when I was yet in my own country; therefore I hastened to flee to Tarshish for I know that You are a gracious G-d and compassionate, slow to anger and abundant in mercy, and relenting of punishing. 3 Therefore now, G-d please take my soul from me for it is better for me to die than to live.' 4 And G-d said: 'Are you so greatly disturbed?' 5 Then Jonah went out of the city and sat on the east side of the city and made himself a booth there and sat under it in it shade until he might see what would become of the city. 6 And G-d prepared a kikayon and made it come up over Jonah, so that it might be a shade over his head to relieve him from his discomfort; and Jonah was very glad because of the kikayon. 7 But G-d prepared a worm at dawn the next day and it attacked the kikayon that it withered. 8 And it was, when the sun arose, that G-d prepared a strong east wind; and the sun beat upon the head of Jonah and he became faint and requested for himself that he might die, and said: 'It is better for me to die than to live.' 9 And G-d said to Jonah: 'Are you so greatly disturbed for the kikayon?' And he said: 'I am greatly disturbed to the point of death.' 10 And G-d said: 'You took pity on the kikayon for which you did not labour nor did you make it grow; which materialised overnight and perished overnight. 11. And I, shall I not take pity upon Nineveh that great city, in which there are more than a hundred and twenty thousand persons who do not know their right hand from their left and many beasts as well?'

Why was Jonah angry?

Jonah observed the immediate repentance of the Ninevites and became very upset for he reasoned that G-d would not now destroy Nineveh. He prayed to G-d and cried out that this was exactly what he had feared would happen, for G-d always accepts sincere repentance. Jonah complained that it would be better for him now to die than to live, to which G-d responded: '... Are you so greatly disturbed?' (v.4)

We will recall that, when Jonah repented inside the fish, he had compared his test to Abraham's test. He had feared the consequences of giving his prophecy just as Abraham feared the consequences of taking Isaac for a sacrifice. Now, however, he can see that this is not so. Abraham's trust in G-d was 'justified' when Isaac was not actually sacrificed. In Jonah's case, however, all his worst fears now seem to have come to pass!

Jonah realises that, if the Ninevites continue to repent, his prophetic warning to them will lead to the Assyrian conquest and exile of the Northern Kingdom. He also fears that he will be denounced as a false prophet for his words will not have come to pass and this will cause a further desecration of G-d's Name among the Assyrians. This is why Jonah now prefers to die. It would have been better for him to have drowned in the sea when thrown overboard by the sailors!

What was the point of G-d's rhetorical question?

G-d's response, however, introduces the narrative that will demonstrate to Jonah that he still misunderstands his role. G-d's question is a rhetorical question. It is as if G-d had said that, in reality, Jonah had absolutely nothing to be disturbed about!

Jonah went out of the city and made himself a hut (Hebrew: Sukkah – possibly a reference to the festival of Sukkot) to shade him from the powerful sun. He sat in its shade to watch what would happen to the city. He was determined to wait for the full forty days, just in case the Ninevites tire of repentance and return to their former ways.

Why was Jonah so pleased with the kikayon?

G-d caused a kikayon (a type of plant) to grow suddenly and to give shade to Jonah for it was extremely hot. Jonah rejoiced at having the kikayon because it gave him shade. Also, however, he took it as a sign from G-d that He would answer his prayers and destroy Nineveh. Jonah assumed that, because G-d performed a miracle for him that was a sign of G-d's pleasure with him. If G-d was pleased with him, consequently, He would certainly answer his prayers.

Early the following morning, however, G-d sent a worm to attack the kikayon so that it withered away and died. When the sun rose, G-d sent a hot east wind and the sun beat down on his head until Jonah was so faint that he asked G-d that he be allowed to die for it was better for him to die than to live.

G-d's final answer to Jonah

G-d asks Jonah if he is so greatly disturbed about the kikayon. Again, this is really a rhetorical question. It is as if G-d is saying that he has no reason to be disturbed about the kikayon. Jonah replies that he is disturbed enough to want to die. G-d's response to this, which is also the last two verses (vv.10-11) of the book, is:

> … You took pity on the kikayon for which you did not labour, nor did you make it grow; which materialised overnight and perished overnight. And I, shall I not take pity upon Nineveh that great city, in which there are more than a hundred and twenty thousand persons who do not know their right hand from their left and many beasts as well.

The point of the kikayon was to demonstrate to Jonah his lack of objectivity. He had done nothing to 'deserve' having the kikayon give him shade since he did not labour over it. He did not complain, however, that he did not deserve it!

When it was taken away from him, however, then he complained! Yet he did not deserve to have it in the first place! His complaint, therefore, demonstrates his, and every human being's, subjectivity. We all look at the world in relation to our own needs and concerns. No person has the ability to understand objectively what is good and bad for the world. G-d alone can understand that.

Jonah has good reasons for not wanting the Ninevites to have the opportunity to repent. When those reasons are removed from consideration, however, all that is left is … a hundred and twenty thousand persons who do not know their right hand from their left and many beasts as well.

How can Jonah know whether there are not other, more important reasons, for the Ninevites being spared? Ultimately, only G-d understands the 'wider picture'. This does not invalidate Jonah's concerns. It simply teaches that G-d's ways are above human understanding and therefore one who has faith in G-d will accept that, even though he does not understand why G-d is doing this, he accepts that G-d's wisdom is ultimately superior and therefore this must be 'for the good'.

COMPARING THE LESSONS IN JOB & JONAH

Job and Jonah were both individuals placed into a situation which they neither understood nor desired. They share the common feature, therefore, that they were both subjected to a form of suffering. But there are many differences between the types of suffering each endured.

SECTION 1:

COMPARING THE OPENING CHAPTERS OF JOB WITH CHAPTER ONE OF JONAH

Job is afflicted with personal physical suffering in that all that is considered valuable or pleasurable in this world [wealth, family and health] are taken away from him.

The reason for the suffering [although unknown to Job] is to test his righteousness. Will he continue to show loyalty to G-d even when he loses everything?

Jonah, by contrast, is challenged with emotional suffering. He is commanded to deliver a prophecy he does not want to give. Jonah's suffering is a consequence of G-d's decision to give Assyria the spiritual advantage that will allow them to conquer and exile the Northern Kingdom of Israel.

Whereas Job's suffering is about him, Jonah's suffering is the anguish he feels about the suffering of others [Israel]. With Job, at no stage does he actually do anything wrong so his suffering is externally afflicted. With Jonah, the more he responds to G-d's instructions in the wrong way, the more suffering he brings upon himself.

Job's response to his suffering is correct at every stage. He accepts the situation of his losses for nothing he lost was ever his in the first place, for everything he ever had possessed was a gift from G-d.

Jonah's response to his suffering is incorrect at every stage, even though his motivation was for the good of others not himself. Jonah rejects his mission and seeks to avert G-d's purpose for he thinks he knows what is for the good.

SECTION 2:

COMPARING THE MESSAGES OF THE COMFORTERS WITH JONAH'S REPENTANCE IN THE BELLY OF THE FISH

In the middle section of Job we have the sequence of the comforters offering explanations of why suffering in this world may occur. Job's comforters fail to present an explanation of Job's suffering that is acceptable to him and, correctly, Job rejects the advice of the comforters.

Through the process of repentance to which he subjects himself in the fish, Jonah finds an explanation for his suffering that is acceptable to him. Even though Jonah has correctly discovered that his initial response to G-d's instruction was wrong, his new 'solution' [comparing himself to Abraham at the binding of Isaac] is still incorrect. Jonah has still failed to accept that G-d has decided it is time for Israel to be punished with exile.

The contrast here is that Job receives answers for his suffering from others and **rejects them correctly**. By comparison, Jonah discovers an answer for his suffering from within himself and accepts it incorrectly.

At this stage, we could take a step back and say that Job was providing an example of the right way to respond to personal suffering whilst Jonah was an example of the wrong way.

SECTION 3:

COMPARING JOB'S REJECTION OF THE COMFORTERS WITH JONAH'S DELIVERING G-D'S MESSAGE TO NINEVEH

In Job's rejection of the comforters we see an individual tortured by his inability to understand what G-d wants of him. Job does not reject his suffering but seeks to understand it and grow from it. He turns to G-d to answer him only because there is nowhere else to turn. Whilst Jonah now accepts his mission from G-d, he does not accept its outcome. Even though, in Chapter 3, Jonah is obeying G-d's instructions, he still wants to fight against G-d's purpose. When he sees the Ninevites repent, he turns to G-d to challenge Him to avert Israel's impending punishment.

SECTION 4:

COMPARING G-D'S FINAL ANSWER TO JOB WITH HIS FINAL ANSWER TO JONAH

In the final section of the book of Job, we finally experience Job being told he is wrong. It is not his place to expect to understand. If G-d is all-wise, then He knows what man needs to know and so if He chooses not to tell man something, it is man's role to accept his ignorance with humility. This is very similar to the answer given to Jonah. Jonah has assumed that anything which will cause Israel not to suffer is good and anything which causes Israel to suffer is evil. G-d challenges Jonah's ability to know this. Only G-d can ultimately know what is really good.

CONCLUSION

Job and Jonah are very different characters set very different tasks. Job has to come to terms with personal loss and suffering whilst Jonah has to battle with the fact that his love and desire for the good of his fellow Jews seems to contradict his responsibilities to G-d.

Ultimately, however, they are both set the same test: to acknowledge the limits of their own ability to understand the ways of G-d. The ultimate lesson for man, be it through the example of Job or Jonah, is to accept in humility the limits of human ability and to have the faith to accept the goodness of G-d simply through the objective rationale that whatever G-d does must ultimately always be good.

THEMES FROM JEWISH SCRIPTURES:

THE PROPHET ELIJAH

1 KINGS 18, 19, 21

CANDIDATES SHOULD BE ABLE TO DEMONSTRATE KNOWLEDGE AND UNDERSTANDING OF:

• THE ROLE OF THE PROPHET AS EXEMPLIFIED BY ELIJAH;

• THE ELIJAH STORIES CONNECTED WITH MOUNT CARMEL, MOUNT HOREB AND NABOTH'S VINEYARD.

CANDIDATES SHOULD BE ABLE TO DISCUSS THESE AREAS CRITICALLY.

INTRODUCTION

The prophet Elijah is first mentioned in the Tenach in I Kings 17 at the beginning of the reign of the wicked Ahab and Jezebel who ruled the Northern Kingdom of Israel during the second half of the eighth century BCE according to the Orthodox chronology of the Tenach. [Scholars of Bible Criticism claim they ruled Israel in the ninth century BCE.]

Ahab was certainly a wicked king. He brought the worship of the Phoenician idol Ba'al into his kingdom. The Talmud[145] credits him, however, as being one who respected Torah scholars. Until he sinned in the incident of Nabot's vineyard (see Chapter 21) Maimonides[146] claims that Ahab's good and bad deeds were equal. The real villain of this period was his wicked wife Jezebel, a Phoenician princess who never abandoned her Phoenician idolatries. It was her influence that induced Ahab to worship Ba'al.

Such was Jezabel's hatred of Judaism that she sought to assassinate every single prophet in Israel.

---

145   TB Sanhedrin 102b
146   Mishnah Torah: Laws of Murderers 4:9

WHO WAS ELIJAH?

The Tenach does not identify Elijah's parents or his tribe. It states in Midrash Rabbah that Elijah is Pinchas, the grandson of Aaron. Pinchas never died but reappeared as Elijah. Even after Elijah ascends to heaven in a fiery chariot,[147] he continues to live, reappearing in every generation to help those who are worthy of him.

Midrash Tanchuma compares Elijah to Moses. G-d redeemed Israel from Egypt through Moses and sustained Israel in every generation through Elijah.[148] There were only two prophets from the tribe of Levi, Moses and Elijah. Just as Moses brought Israel out of Egypt and they never returned, so when Elijah heralds the Messianic redemption, Israel will never again return to exile. The Midrash lists many more similarities between them.

There is also a Talmudic tradition that Elijah attends every Brit Milah ceremony and that is why the chair that the Sandek sits on is called Elijah's chair. There is also a tradition that, at the Pesach Seder, the fifth cup of wine, which is poured but not drunk, is called Elijah's cup. The prophet Malachi[149] states that, at the end of days, Elijah will herald the imminent arrival of the Messiah.

---

147   II Kings 2:1-12
148   Based on Hosea 12:14
149   Malachi 3:23

I KINGS 17

At the beginning of Ahab's reign, Israel enjoyed a period of great material prosperity. This might have been the cause of the laxity that led to the spreading of Ba'al-worship in the land. In Elijah's first meeting with Ahab, he warns him that there would be a drought and only through his word would the rain fall.

Why was Elijah so harsh with Ahab at this time?

The Talmud[150] explains that Elijah and Ahab had both gone to comfort Chiel, whose sons died when he attempted to rebuild Jericho[151], in line with the curse issued by Joshua.

Ahab taunted Elijah saying: the curse of the student was fulfilled but not the curse of the teacher. By this, he meant that the curse of Joshua, the student, was fulfilled when all Chiel's sons died, but the curse of Moses, that the heavens would be closed up if Israel worshipped idols[152], had not been fulfilled. Immediately, Elijah responded that there would be a drought. Elijah wanted the people to respond to the drought by repenting and turning away from idolatry.

Once the drought began, Elijah was forced to flee. G-d guided Elijah to a brook where he was sustained by ravens that miraculously brought him food to eat.

Why was Elijah sustained in this way?

Malbim suggests that while Israel suffered a drought it was inappropriate for Elijah to have rain, so G-d guided him to a brook. Metzudat David adds that ravens are naturally cruel birds and this was a hint to Elijah that he should also show mercy to Israel and not extend the drought.

---

150   TB Sanhedrin 113a
151   Recorded at the end of I Kings 16
152   See Deuteronomy 11:15

Elijah goes to Tzarfat

When the water in the brook dried up, Elijah went to the city of Tzarfat where he requested a little water from a widow gathering wood. The widow gave him water but when he also asked for something to eat she cried that she had only sufficient for her and her son. Elijah performed a miracle for her and the containers of flour and oil that she had did not cease to be full. Her son then became ill and appeared to have died but Elijah resuscitated him. Some say he actually died and Elijah brought him back to life. There is a Talmudic tradition[153] that the widow's son grew up to be the prophet Jonah.

How was Elijah able to revive the widow's son?

The Talmud states Elijah was able to cause the drought for he prayed that G-d loan him the Key of Rains. When the boy died, Elijah prayed that G-d loan him the Key of Resurrecting the Dead. G-d replied that there were only three keys in heaven (the other one was the Key of Childbirth) and it would not be right for Elijah to have two keys and G-d to have only one. He would only loan him the Key of Resurrecting the Dead if Elijah returned the Key of Rains. This Elijah did and the drought was ended.

---

153   TB Sanhedrin 113a

I KINGS 18

ELIJAH CHALLENGES THE PRIESTS OF BA'AL

1 And it was after many days that the word of G-d came to Elijah in the third year saying: Go and show yourself to Ahab and I will send rain upon the land. *2* So Elijah went to show himself to Ahab and the famine was severe in Samaria. *3* Then Ahab called Obadiah who was over the household; now Obadiah feared G-d greatly. *4* For it was when Jezebel cut off the prophets of G-d that Obadiah took a hundred prophets and hid fifty of them in a cave and fed them bread and water. *5* And Ahab said to Obadiah: go through the land to all the springs of water and to all the brooks, perhaps we shall find grass and save the lives of the horses and mules that we not lose all the beasts. *6* So they divided the land between them to pass through it; Ahab went one way by himself and Obadiah went another way by himself. *7* Now Obadiah was on the road and suddenly Elijah was in front of him; he recognised him, fell on his face and said: Is it you, my lord Elijah? *8* And he answered him: It is I; go, tell your master: behold, Elijah is here. *9* And he said: How have I sinned that you have delivered your servant into the hand of Ahab, to slay me? *10* As the Lord your G-d lives, there is no nation or kingdom where my master has not sent to seek you; and when they said: he is not here, he took an oath of the kingdom and nation, that they had not found you. *11* And now you say: Go, tell your master: behold, Elijah is here. *12* And it will be, as soon as I am gone from you, that the spirit of G-d will carry you I know not where; and so when I come and tell Ahab and he cannot find you, he will slay me; but I your servant have feared G-d from my youth. *13* Was it not told my master what I did when Jezebel killed the prophets of G-d, how I hid a hundred men, G-d's prophets, fifty in a cave and fed them bread and water? *14* And now you say: go tell your master: behold, Elijah is here; and he will slay me. *15* And Elijah said: As the G-d of hosts lives, before whom I stand, I will surely show myself to him today. *16* So Obadiah went to meet Ahab and told him and Ahab went to meet Elijah. *17* And it was when Ahab saw Elijah that Ahab said to him: 'Is it you, who brings troubles on Israel? *18* And he answered: I have not troubled Israel but you and your father's house, in that you have forsaken G-d's commandments and have followed the Baalim. *19* Now therefore send and gather all Israel to Mount Carmel and four hundred and fifty prophets of Baal and four hundred prophets of the Asherah that eat at Jezebel's table. *20* So Ahab sent to all the children of Israel and gathered the prophets together to Mount Carmel. *21* Then Elijah came near to all the people and said: For how long shall you hop between two views, if the Lord be G-d, follow Him, but if Baal, then follow him; and the people answered him not a word. *22* Then said Elijah to the people: I alone am left a prophet of G-d, but Baal's prophets are four hundred and fifty men. *23* Let them therefore give us two bulls and let them choose one bull for themselves and cut it in pieces and lay it on the wood and put no fire under; and I will dress the other bull and lay it on the wood and put no fire under. *24* And you will call in the name of your god and I will call in the name of G-d and the G-d that answers by fire, He shall truly be G-d; and all the people answered and said: It is well spoken. *25* Then Elijah said to the prophets of Baal: Choose one bull for yourselves *and prepare it first for you are many; and call on the name of your god but put no fire under. 26 And they took the bull which was given them and they prepared it and called on the name of Baal from morning until noon saying: O Baal, answer us; but there was no voice nor any that answered: and they danced and hopped about the altar which they made. 27 And it was at noon that Elijah mocked them, and said: cry louder for he is a god; either he is talking, or he is chasing [enemies] or he is on a journey or perhaps he is sleeping and must be woken. 28 And they cried louder and cut themselves after their manner with swords and lances until the blood gushed out from them. 29 And as the afternoon passed, they attempted to prophesise until the time of the evening offering, but there was neither voice nor answer nor anyone that heard. 30 And Elijah said to all the people: come near to me, and all the people came near to him; then he repaired the altar of G-d that was torn down. 31 Then Elijah took twelve stones, according to the number of the tribes of the sons of Jacob, to whom the word of G-d came saying: Israel shall be your name. 32 And with the stones he built an altar in the name of G-d; and he made a trench around the altar as great as would contain two measures of seed. 33 And he put the wood in order and cut the bull in pieces and laid it on the wood. 34 And he said: Fill me four pitchers with water and pour them on the burnt-offering and on the wood; and he said: Do it a second time, and they did it a second time; and he said: Do it a third time, and they did it a third time. 35 And the water ran around the altar, and he filled the trench also with water. 36 And it was at the time of the evening offering that Elijah the prophet came near and said: O G-d, the G-d of Abraham, Isaac and Israel: let it be known this day that You are G-d in Israel and that I am Your servant and that I have done all these things by Your word. 37 Answer me G-d answer me that this people may know that You, G-d, are G-d, for You did turn their hearts backwards. 38 Then the fire of G-d fell and consumed the burnt-offering and the wood and the stones and the dust and licked up the water that was in the trench. 39 And when all the people saw it, they fell on their faces and they said: G-d He is G-d, G-d He is G-d. 40 And Elijah said to them: Take the prophets of Baal, let not one of them escape; and they took them and Elijah brought them down to brook Kishon and smote them there. 41 And Elijah said to Ahab: get up, eat and drink for there is the rumbling sound of the rain. 42 So Ahab went up to eat and drink and Elijah went up to the top of Carmel; and he bowed down upon the earth and put his face between his knees. 43 And he said to his servant: Go up now, look toward the sea; and he went up and looked, and said: There is nothing; and he said: Go again seven times. 44 And it was on the seventh time that he said: Behold, a cloud arises out of the sea as small as a man's palm; and he said: go up, say unto Ahab: Make ready [your chariot] and come down, lest the rain stop you. 45 And it was in a little while that the heaven grew dark with clouds and wind, and there was a heavy rain; and Ahab rode and went to Jezreel. 46 And the hand of G-d was on Elijah and he girded his loins and ran before Ahab until coming to Jezreel.*

In the third year of the famine, G-d instructs Elijah to go to Ahab and set in motion the means for ending the famine. Now Ahab had appointed the prophet Obadiah over his household. This is the same Obadiah listed as one of the Twelve Minor Prophets.

WHY DID THE WICKED AHAB APPOINT SUCH A RIGHTEOUS MAN OVER HIS HOUSEHOLD?

The Talmud[154] explains that Ahab reasoned that the wicked Laban had been blessed because he appointed Jacob over his household and the immoral Potiphar had been blessed because he appointed the righteous Joseph over his household. Perhaps he too would be blessed if he appointed the righteous Obadiah over his house!

In fact, it was Obadiah who risked his life to save a hundred prophets from Jezebel when she wanted to kill all the prophets in Israel. He hid them in two caves, fifty in each, reasoning that if one cave was discovered at least the others would be spared.

WHY DID JEZEBEL WANT TO KILL ALL THE PROPHETS?

She was a committed idolater and so she could not stand the integrity of G-d's prophets, who would never acknowledge her idols, no matter how powerful she was.

ELIJAH APPEARS TO OBADIAH

Meanwhile, Ahab and Obadiah went in search of pasture for their animals in the famine. Ahab decided they should split up and go in opposite directions. When Obadiah was alone, Elijah appeared to him and told him to inform his master (Ahab) that he was here and would await him.

Obadiah feared doing what Elijah said because Ahab hated Elijah and would want to kill him if he had a chance. The Talmud[155] states that Ahab had sent messengers to many lands in search of Elijah but none had found him. Surely Elijah would not stay around to be killed by Ahab? Then, when Ahab arrived and found Elijah not there, he would blame Obadiah for wasting his time and have Obadiah put to death! [Some say Obadiah was not just concerned for himself. If he was put to death, who would care for the hidden prophets?]

154   TB Sanhedrin 39b
155   TB Megillah 11b

ELIJAH CHALLENGES AHAB

Elijah assured Obadiah that he would stay and so Obadiah went to tell Ahab. When he arrived, Ahab accused Elijah of bringing trouble to Israel for it was he who had decreed the famine. Elijah replied by saying that the famine was caused by Ahab and his family for their idol-worship and their disregard for G-d's commandments.

Elijah challenged Ahab to gather all Israel to Mount Carmel if he wanted the famine to end. He was also to summon 450 prophets of Baal and 400 prophets of Asheirah ... who eat at Jezebel's table. (v. 19) This was a reference to the most powerful priests who enjoyed the Queen's favour. Ahab duly organized this meeting, to which the people came enthusiastically.

WHY DID ELIJAH ONLY CONFRONT BA'AL'S PROPHETS?

In the end, Elijah only confronted the prophets of Ba'al and not Asheirah. Some say that was because the worship of Asheirah was much more degenerate than the worship of Ba'al and the people knew that this was wrong so Elijah ignored them. Others say that the prophets of Asheirah did not turn up. They were particularly close to Jezebel and she would not let them attend.

THE CHALLENGE AT MOUNT CARMEL

Elijah first addressed the people and told them they had to decide. Either they worship G-d or they worship Ba'al but they cannot worship both. The people did not know what to believe and so Elijah set the test. Both he and the priests of Ba'al would build altars and slaughter a sacrifice. After placing the sacrifice on the altar they would call out for their sacrifice to be accepted. A fire would come down from heaven and consume the 'accepted' sacrifice and in this way they would know who was worthy of their worship.

Elijah emphasises that he is but one prophet and the Ba'al has 450 prophets. Yet he was confident that his prayers would outweigh the 450. Elijah offered the prophets of Ba'al to go first. Two bulls would be selected and they could choose which one they wanted. Abarbanel points out that, in the world of idolatory, Ba'al represented the Sun (some say the prophet Mars) which controls all heat. So Elijah even made the terms of the test something which should, as it were, give Ba'al an advantage!

Elijah, of course, knew that G-d showed His acceptance of sacrifices in the Temple by sending a fire down to consume it and he was confident his sacrifice would be accepted. The people, however, being of the Northern Kingdom, had not visited the Temple in Jerusalem for generations and this had been forgotten by them.

THE PRIESTS OF BA'AL OFFER THEIR SACRIFICE

The people accepted the fairness of the challenge and the bulls were selected. The prophets of Ba'al chose the choicer bull and prepared it, chanting and praying to Ba'al from morning until noon, imploring Ba'al to answer them. They performed all their ritual dances as well but, of course, there was no answer.

When noon arrived and still there was no answer, Elijah scoffed at the priests of Ba'al. Noon, of course, is the time when the sun is at its height, a most appropriate time for a sun-god to answer one's prayers!

Elijah taunted them, suggesting they should shout louder in case Ba'al was asleep or busy attending to some other need! At this point, the priests cut themselves for they believed the sight of the redness of their blood might cause their prayers to be answered. They continued their imploring Ba'al through the afternoon until they were totally exhausted. It says that ...none answered because none heard (verse 29) indicating that there was no such being as Ba'al, it did not exist at all.

ELIJAH OFFERS HIS SACRIFICE

Elijah then bade the people gather around as he fixed the broken altar used for sacrifices to G-d. Rashi states that it was the altar originally built by King Saul. When the Northern Kingdom split from Judah, their king, Jeroboam, set up golden calves in Dan and Beit-El and destroyed all the altars. Some say Elijah told the people to come closer so there would be no suspicion he was doing any deception.

Elijah took twelve stones, corresponding to the twelve sons of Jacob, so that he be answered in their merit. He then made an altar with these stones. He then dug a trench around the altar before arranging the altar with the wood and the meat upon it.

He ordered that four pitchers of water be brought and poured over the sacrifice. This was done a second and third time and the trench was then filled with water. Redak points out that twelve pitchers of water were poured on the altar corresponding to the twelve tribes and that they were poured in three groups, corresponding to the three patriarchs, in whose merit he should be answered. This demonstrates the humility of Elijah, who did not rely on his own worth for G-d to answer him.

As evening approached, Elijah prayed that G-d answer him so that all will know that He alone is G-d. A fire then came down from the sky and consumed the sacrifice. When the people saw this they fell on their faces and said The Lord is [truly] G-d (verse 39). This statement of faith is chanted seven times at the end of the Yom Kippur service.

HOW CAN SACRIFICES BE OFFERED OUTSIDE THE TEMPLE?

Once the Temple was built, it was now forbidden to build altars and offer sacrifices anywhere else. How could Elijah do this? There are two answers to this question:

ANSWER ONE

Some say Elijah received a specific command from G-d to do this as it was an exceptional situation so the regular laws could be set aside.

ANSWER TWO

Others say there was no command. Elijah himself realized that this was an exceptional situation and so the regular laws could be set aside.

Either way, this is an example of the principle that there are times when the law can be set aside. For example, if somebody's life is in danger, and it is Shabbat, one may (in fact, one must) break Shabbat if that is necessary to help them. Similarly, when the Rabbis realised the Oral Law might be forgotten, they overrode the prohibition against writing down the Oral Law. Elijah was doing the same thing here. In order to prevent idolatry, he overrode the law against offering sacrifices outside the Temple.

THE PEOPLE TURN AGAINST BA'AL

When the people saw what had happened, they turned against the priests of Ba'al. They captured them, took them down to the Kishon brook and there they executed them all.

THE END OF THE FAMINE

Elijah now turns to Ahab and tells him to return home for the rains are coming and the famine has ended. He sent a servant to look out to sea but he saw nothing. After sending him seven times, he reported that there was a cloud the size of a man's hand rising from the sea. Elijah bade them return home quickly lest the rain overtake them. Meanwhile, the cloud grew and the heavens darkened. Soon heavy rain was falling and, despite the fact Ahab rode on a horse, Elijah ran before him all the way to Jezreel.

Most commentaries connect the people forsaking idolatry with the end of the famine. This whole challenge to the priests of Ba'al was in order that the people would merit the end of the famine.

I KINGS 19

ELIJAH

&

THE

STILL

SMALL

VOICE

1 And Ahab told Jezebel all that Elijah had done and how he had slain all the prophets with the sword. 2 Then Jezebel sent a messenger to Elijah, saying: 'So let the gods do to me and more also if I make not your life as the life of one of them by this time tomorrow.' 3 And he saw and arose and went for his life and came to Beersheba which belonged to Judah, and left his servant there. 4 But he himself went a day's journey into the wilderness and came and sat down under a juniper and requested for himself that he might die; and said: 'It is enough; now, O G-d take away my life for I am not better than my fathers.' 5 And he lay down and slept under a juniper and behold an angel touched him, and said to him: 'Arise and eat.' 6 And he looked and behold there was at his head a cake baked on hot coals and a flask of water; he ate and drank and lay down again. 7 And the angel of G-d returned a second time and touched him and said: 'Arise and eat; because the journey is too much for you.' 8 And he arose and ate and drank and went with the strength of that meal forty days and forty nights to Horeb, the mountain of G-d. 9 And he came there to the cave and lodged there and behold, the word of G-d came to him, and He said to him: 'What are you doing here, Elijah?' 10 And he said: 'I have been zealous for G-d, the G-d of hosts, for the children of Israel have forsaken Your covenant, torn down Your altars and slain Your prophets with the sword; and I alone am left and they seek my life, to take it away.' 11 And He said: 'Go out and stand on the mountain before G-d.'; behold G-d passed by, and a great and strong wind splits the mountains and shatters boulders before G-d but G-d was not in the wind; and after the wind an earthquake; but G-d was not in the earthquake. 12 And after the earthquake a fire but G-d was not in the fire; and after the fire a still small voice. 13 And it was when Elijah heard it that he wrapped his face in his mantle and went out and stood in the entrance of the cave and a voice came to him, and said: 'What are you doing here, Elijah?' 14 And he said: 'I have been zealous for G-d, the G-d of hosts; for the children of Israel have forsaken Your covenant, torn down Your altars and slain your prophets with the sword; and I alone am left and they seek my life, to take it away.' 15 And G-d said to him: 'Go, return on your way to the wilderness of Damascus and you shall come and anoint Hazael to be king over Aram. 16 and Jehu the son of Nimshi shall you anoint king over Israel and Elisha the son of Shaphat of Abel-meholah shall you anoint to be prophet after you. 17 And it shall be that he that escapes the sword of Hazael shall Jehu slay; and he that escapes the sword of Jehu shall Elisha slay. 18 I shall leave seven thousand in Israel, all the knees which have not bowed to Baal and every mouth which has not kissed him.' 19 So he went from there and found Elisha the son of Shaphat who was ploughing with twelve yoke before him, and he was with the twelfth; and Elijah went over to him and threw his mantle over him. 20 And he left the oxen and ran after Elijah, saying: 'Please let me kiss my father and mother, and then I will follow you'; and he said to him: 'Go back for what have I done to you?' 21 And he returned from following him and took the yoke and slaughtered them and with the gear of the oxen cooked their flesh and gave the people and they ate; he then arose and followed Elijah, and ministered to him.

JEZEBEL SWEARS REVENGE AGAINST ELIJAH

When Ahab returned, he told Jezebel everything that Elijah had done: how he had miraculously brought a fire down from heaven and how he had caused all the priests of Ba'al to be executed. Jezebel was furious and sent a message to Elijah, making an oath in the name of her idols, that she would see to it that Elijah would die for this. Elijah recognized the danger and immediately fled for his life. He initially sought refuge in Beersheba, which was in the southern kingdom of Judea.

WHY DID ELIJAH RUN AWAY AND NOT TRUST IN G-D?

The commentaries give two different answers: ANSWER 1:

G-d expects us to do everything we can to save ourselves and not rely on miracles. Only after we have done everything we can and are still in danger might G-d perform a miracle.

ANSWER 2

G-d had just performed a miracle for Elijah when he sent the fire down to accept his sacrifice on Mount Carmel. Elijah was afraid he didn't deserve another so soon afterwards.

ELIJAH GOES INTO THE DESERT

Even though he was probably safe in Beersheba, Elijah did not want to take a chance that somebody might betray him and deliver him into the hands of Jezebel. He went out into the desert where nobody would find him. Abarbanel suggests he sought rest under a juniper tree because it repels poisonous insects and reptiles. Elijah requested to die because it was better to die at the hand of G-d in the desert than to be executed by Jezebel.

AN ANGEL COMES TO ELIJAH

Elijah lay down to sleep and an angel awakened him three times and bade him eat and drink. Miraculously, Elijah found a cake baked on hot coals and a flask of water had been provided for him. The angel told Elijah he was to go on a long journey and, after eating for the third time, Elijah was strengthened to not need food again for forty days and forty nights. Elijah followed the route set for him by the angel and had no idea where he was going. He eventually arrived at Mount Horeb which, according to Jewish tradition, is another name for Mount Sinai.

G-D SPEAKS TO ELIJAH

Elijah lodged in a cave in the mountain when suddenly the voice of G-d came to him and asked him what he was doing there! Some interpret this question as a criticism of Elijah, for he had abandoned his people to seek safety for himself. Others say G-d was merely opening a conversation with him in the way He did with Adam.

Immediately, Elijah defends himself. He claims that it is impossible for him to remain in the northern kingdom, where G-d's covenant had been abandoned, His altars had been torn down, all the prophets except him had been murdered and now Jezebel wanted to murder him too.

Some say that, when Elijah said that G-d's covenant had been abandoned, he was referring to the covenant of circumcision. In this he was wrong, for the people never abandoned this covenant. Elijah's punishment for this slander was that, until the end of time, he would be present at every circumcision to testify that he was wrong to say this about Israel!

ELIJAH HAS THE VISION OF THE STILL SMALL VOICE

Elijah was told to stand before G-d on the mountain and witness a vision of G-d. There was a mighty wind that was so strong it could split mountains and shatter boulders, but G-d was not in the wind. After the wind, there was an earthquake but G-d was not in the earthquake. After the earthquake there was a fire but G-d was not in the fire. After the fire there was a still, small voice.

The image of the still, small voice is explained as an image of where real power lays. Those who are weak give an impression of strength by making a lot of noise, like the earthquake and the fire. The one who has real strength does not need to prove his strength. His quiet confidence carries the message across.

Another explanation describes the still, small voice as the voice of praise and gentle encouragement which achieves far more than brute force. The wind, earthquake and fire are all forces of destruction, but G-d does not exert His power by punishing but by encouraging the sinner to repent.

Yet another explanation relates these four images to Israel's punishments: The wind is Egypt against whom none could stand until G-d brought His plagues. The earthquake is Babylon who shattered the foundations of Israel's false sense of security that the Temple could never be destroyed. The fire is Rome who ended Israel's connection to their land and began the long exile. The still, small voice is G-d's concealed presence in the exile. He is there, protecting His people still, but He is not noticed.

G-D SPEAKS TO ELIJAH AGAIN
Elijah hides his face from the vision and G-d asks him again what he is doing here and Elijah answers again that G-d's covenant had been abandoned, His altars had been torn down, all the prophets except him had been murdered and now Jezebel wanted to murder him too.

WHY DID G-D SPEAK TO ELIJAH AGAIN?
There are two different opinions about this:

Some say Elijah was being punished for abandoning his people. When G-d asked him this question again he should have responded by asking G-d to forgive His people as Moses had done.

Others say that Elijah was being rewarded for sanctifying G-d's Name at Mount Carmel and executing the priests of Ba'al. Only Moses had merited seeing G-d's 'still small voice' on Mount Sinai. Elijah was being given a great privilege

G-D PREPARES THE MEANS TO PUNISH ISRAEL
G-d then tells Elijah to return by the way in which he came and to anoint Hazael to be king over Aram and Jehu to be king over Israel. He is also told to anoint Elisha to be a prophet after him.

According to those who say Elijah was being punished, G-d has terminated his career as a prophet and instructed him to anoint Elisha to replace him.

According to those who say Elijah was being rewarded, he had now earned the right to ascend to heaven in a fiery chariot and therefore had to appoint a successor to continue his work on earth.

Those whom Hazael failed to kill would be killed by Jehu and those who Jehu failed to kill would be killed by Elisha. Actually, it was Elisha who anointed these kings[156] but it was in Elijah's merit that he fulfilled his teacher's task.

The point of these anointments was that G-d would fulfill Elijah's request that the wicked be punished. Jehu wiped out the entire family of Ahab, including Jezebel[157] and Hazael (who ruled Aram in the days of Jehu's son) also killed many in Israel. There is no indication of Elisha killing anybody directly, but some say that when Elisha would rebuke the people and they did not listen to him, Israel's enemies attacked and killed many people. It was as if Elisha's words had killed them. G-d tells Elijah that only seven thousand will remain in Israel, the only ones who did not worship Ba'al at all.

Elijah returned and found Elisha ploughing for his father. He was on the twelfth plough when Elijah threw his mantle over him. This symbolized Elijah's desire for Elisha to become his disciple. Elisha requested that he be allowed to embrace his parents before following Elijah. Elisha then prepared a feast with the oxen before going after Elijah.

WHAT IS THE SIGNIFICANCE OF THE TWELVE PLOUGHS?
There are two explanations of this:

Some say it indicates that Elisha would be a prophet to all the twelve tribes of Israel.

Others say it indicates the great wealth of his family. He nevertheless gave up this wealth to become a disciple of Elijah.

Elisha made a feast to celebrate the great joy he felt at becoming the disciple of Elijah, the greatest prophet of his generation.

---

156   see II Kings 9
157   see II Kings 9-10

I KINGS 20

AHAB ATTEMPTS TO MAINTAIN PEACE WITH ARAM

Following these events, Ben-Hadad, the king of Aram, massed an army against Israel. He sent messengers to Ahab demanding a tribute of his silver, gold, wives and children. Ahab thought this was just a show of strength to impress his allies and so he agreed. Ben-Hadad then sent back messengers demanding all of Ahab's silver, gold, wives and children!

Ahab summoned the Sages who advised him to resist Ben-Hadad. There are many different opinions as to what exactly Ben-Hadad wanted but all agree that Ahab was praised in this incident for respecting and following the advice of the Torah scholars. His further attempts to appease Ben-Hadad all fail and eventually Ben-Hadad lays a siege upon Ahab.

WAR WITH ARAM

In order to break the siege, Ahab is advised by a prophet, some say this was Michayahu (not to be mixed up with Micah) to select 232 young men to attack Ben-Haddad's troops. The prophet assured Ahab that G-d would deliver his enemies into his hands. Ahab did as instructed and the army of Aram fled from before him as Ahab scored a notable victory. Ben-Hadad managed to escape but Ahab was warned that he would return the following year to do battle with Ahab again.

A SECOND WAR WITH ARAM

Ben-Hadad, was advised that he had lost because he fought on the mountains where Israel's G-d was powerful. He would be victorious if he fought Israel in the plains. So the following year Ben-Hadad returned with a very powerful army, far outnumbering Israel's army and encamped at Aphek in the plain. The prophet assured Ahab that, since Ben-Hadad was convinced that G-d was powerful only in the mountains, Aram would be delivered into their hands in the valley. After a seven-day standoff, Israel attacked and killed 100,000 of Aram. The rest of their army fled to the city.

AHAB SPARES BEN-HADAD

The remnant of Aram's army, together with Ben-Hadad sought refuge, donned sackcloth and ashes and begged forgiveness, trusting in the kindliness of Israel's king. Ahab had mercy on Ben-Hadad, who promised him great wealth form Damascus in return.

PROPHECY OF AHAB'S DEATH

Ahab was reproved by the prophet for sparing Ben-Hadad's life. Ahab was now told he would be put to death. The commentaries compare Ahab's misplaced mercy with that of King Saul, who spared Agag, the king of Amalek, for which he was stripped of the kingdom.

Some say Ahab only spared Ben-Hadad in order to accumulate wealth for himself. Others say he should have realised that, when G-d caused so many to die miraculously in battle, it was obviously the will of G-d that the king of Aram should die as well. Ahab should have realised this.

I KINGS 21

AHAB
&
THE
VINEYARD
OF

NABOTH

1 And it was after these things, that Naboth the Jezreelite had a vineyard in Jezreel by the palace of Ahab, king of Samaria. *2* And Ahab spoke to Naboth saying: 'Give me your vineyard, that I may have it for a vegetable garden since it is near to my house; and I will give you for it a better vineyard; or, if it pleases you, I will give you its worth in money.' *3* And Naboth said to Ahab: 'G-d forbid that I should give the inheritance of my fathers to you.' *4* And Ahab came into his house sad and upset because of the words which Naboth the Jezreelite had spoken to him and said: 'I will not give you the inheritance of my fathers;' and he laid down upon his bed and turned away his face and would eat no bread.

5 But Jezebel his wife came to him, and said to him: 'Why is your spirit so sad that you eat no bread?' *6* And he said to her: 'For I spoke to Naboth the Jezreelite and said to him: Give me your vineyard for money or if you prefer I will give you another vineyard for it; and he answered: 'I will not give you my vineyard.' *7* And Jezebel his wife said to him: 'Do you now govern the kingdom of Israel: arise, and eat bread and let your heart be merry; I will give you the vineyard of Naboth the Jezreelite. *8* So she wrote letters in Ahab's name and sealed them with his seal and sent the letters to the elders and to the nobles that were in his city who sat with Naboth. *9* And she wrote in the letters saying: 'Proclaim a fast and set Naboth at the head of the people. *10* And set two wicked men before him to testify against him, saying: You have cursed G-d and the king; and then remove him and stone him that he die.'

11 And the men of his city, the elders and the nobles who dwelt in his city, did as Jezebel had sent to them, as was written in the letters she had sent to them. *12* They proclaimed a fast and set Naboth at the head of the people. *13* And two wicked men came and sat before him; and the wicked men testified against Naboth in front of the people saying: 'Naboth cursed G-d and the king;' then they took him out of the city and stoned him with stones and he died. *14* Then they sent to Jezebel, saying: 'Naboth was stoned and is dead.'

15 And it was when Jezebel heard that Naboth was stoned and was dead that Jezebel said to Ahab: 'Arise, take possession of the vineyard of Naboth the Jezreelite, which he refused to give you for money, for Naboth is not alive but dead.' *16* And it was when Ahab heard that Naboth was dead that Ahab arose to go down to the vineyard of Naboth the Jezreelite, to take possession of it.

17 And the word of G-d came to Elijah the Tishbite, saying: *18* 'Arise, go down to Ahab king of Israel who is in Samaria; behold, he is in Naboth's vineyard where he has gone down to take possession of it. *19* And you shall speak to him, saying: Thus says G-d: Have you murdered and also inherited; and you shall speak to him, saying: Thus says G-d: 'in the place where dogs licked the blood of Naboth shall dogs lick your blood, even yours.'

20 And Ahab said to Elijah: 'Have you found me, my enemy?' and he answered: 'I have found you because you have allowed yourself to do that which is evil in the sight of G-d. *21* I will bring disaster upon you and will utterly sweep you away, and will cut off from Ahab every male child and those that are bound and those that are free in Israel. *22* And I will make your house like the house of Jeroboam the son of Nebat, and like the house of Basha the son of Ahijah, for the anger in that you have angered Me, and caused Israel to sin. *23* And of Jezebel G-d also spoke saying: 'The dogs shall eat Jezebel in the valley of Jezreel. *24* The dead of Ahab in the city the dogs shall eat and the dead in the field shall the birds of the air eat.' *25* For there was none like Ahab who sold himself to do evil in the eyes of G-d, for Jezebel his wife had incited him. *26* And he did very abominably in following idols, as the Amorites did, whom G-d had cast out from before the children of Israel. *27* And it was when Ahab heard these words that he tore his clothes and put on sackcloth and fasted and lay in sackcloth, and went slowly.

28 And the word of G-d came to Elijah the Tishbite, saying: *29* 'See how Ahab humbles himself before Me; because he humbles himself before Me, I will not bring the evil in his days but in his son's days will I bring the disaster upon his house.'

AHAB HAD NO RIGHT TO NABOTH'S VINEYARD

Ahab had a palace in Jezreel and Naboth's vineyard adjoined the palace. A king has a right to demand fields and vineyards. This was one of the things Samuel warned the people about before they appointed King Saul.[158] The Talmud explains, however, that this only applies outside the town. Naboth's vineyard was inside the city boundary and so Ahab was not entitled to take it for himself.

Some say that a king is only entitled to take the produce but not the actual land as Ahab wanted to do. Others say that the rights of kings only apply to rightful kings, descended from King David. Ahab ruled the Northern Kingdom and so perhaps these privileges did not apply to him at all!

WHY DID NABOTH REFUSE TO SELL?

Ahab said he wanted to cut down the vine and plant vegetables. The Torah forbids cutting down a fruit tree. Also, Naboth knew Ahab would erect a shrine to Ba'al in the vineyard. This is what Naboth meant (v. 3) when he said: G-d forbid that I should give the inheritance of my fathers to you. G-d would not permit him to sell the vineyard.

WHY WAS AHAB SO UPSET ABOUT THIS?

Ahab had been rebuked by Naboth and was ashamed. He only told Jezebel that he was angry with Naboth for not selling, but deep down he knew he was in the wrong.

JEZEBEL TAKES CONTROL

Although Ahab was a sinner, this only stemmed from his weakness and his inability to control his desires. Jezebel, on the other hand, was really wicked. She scolded Ahab for being so soft with Naboth. How dare he refuse the king? She vowed to avenge his 'honour' which had been 'offended' by this man.

JEZEBEL PLANS NABOTH'S EXECUTION

Jezebel sent letters instructing the Elders (who were intimidated by her as well) to proclaim a fast day, as if some great sin had been committed. Then they were to accuse Naboth by having two false witnesses claim they saw Naboth curse G-d and the king. The people would be outraged and assume the accusations were true and they would demand Naboth be executed.

---

158   see I Samuel 8:14

It is interesting to note that Jezebel had to have Naboth put on trial and convicted of a crime. She could not just have him murdered. This indicates how strong the rule of law was even at this time. Also, even confirmed idolaters like Ahab and Jezebel considered blasphemy (taking G-d's Name in vain) a capital crime. This shows that they only worshipped idols in order to satisfy their desires. They knew, deep down, that G-d was there.

WHY ALSO ACCUSE NABOTH OF CURSING THE KING?
Naboth could have been executed just for blasphemy, but by adding the crime of cursing the king, Naboth has also committed treason. When somebody is convicted of treason, his property can be taken away by the king. Had Naboth just been accused of blasphemy, his children would have inherited his property. So now Ahab gets Naboth's vineyard 'legally' and without paying for it!

ELIJAH DELIVERS G-D'S CURSE TO AHAB
G-d now instructs Elijah to go down to Ahab and reprove him for his actions. First he colludes in Naboth's murder then he 'inherits' his vineyard as if he were a grieving son! In verse 19, the phrase: and you shall speak to him, saying appears twice. First Elijah reproves Ahab and then waits to see if Ahab confesses or shows remorse. When neither happened, Elijah continued with the curse that where the dogs licked the blood of Naboth, there they would also lick the blood of Ahab.[159]

Many commentaries claim that, when he heard the curse, Ahab's response in verse 20 indicates that he tried to defend himself. They suggest he claimed that it was all Jezebel's doing and he knew nothing of it. But Elijah dismissed this completely. The specifics of how it was done may have been thought up by Jezebel, but it was all done with Ahab's approval and desire.

Elijah continues G-d's curse that every male descendant of Ahab will die so that there will be no remnant of his name in Israel at all. Some say the curse also included the loss of all his possessions. Others say the curse included Ahab losing his portion in the next world.[160]

---

159   This prophecy was fulfilled when Ahab was slain in battle
by the army of Aram. See 22:38 for details.
160   Ahab is one of those mentioned in the Talmudic debate concerning those who lost their
portion in the World-to-Come. See TB Sanhedrin 102b.

The curse concludes that Jezebel's body would be eaten by dogs in the valley of Jezreel. The dead of Ahab in the house would also be eaten by dogs and the dead of the field would be eaten by the birds.

AHAB DONS SACKCLOTH AND FASTS
When Ahab heard these words he was totally shocked and immediately tore his garments and put on sackcloth. He also fasted and lay in a bed of sackcloth. The Talmud[161] points out that it does not say Ahab showed remorse or that he repented. Ahab's response was motivated by fear of punishment rather than a genuine remorse for his actions. Nevertheless, G-d spared him for his actions and postponed the judgement against him. The destruction of the house of Ahab would not happen until the days of his son.

---

161 TB Sanhedrin 90a